HOUSES AND (
OF CORNWALL

A Personal Choice

by

Helen McCabe

TABB HOUSE

First published 1988
Tabb House, 7 Church Street, Padstow, Cornwall, PL28 8BG

New edition 1996

ISBN 1 873951 221

Printed in Great Britain by The Short Run Press Ltd, Exeter, Devon

Contents

Foreword

BY the eleventh century Cornwall was divided into districts known as Hundreds. The maps in John Norden's *Description of Cornwall* compiled in the early seventeenth century show nine divisions very clearly. *Stratton, Lesnewth, Trigg,* and *Pydar* run from the Tamar and Devon border down the north coast of Cornwall to *Penwith* in the extreme south west. *Kerrier, Powder, West,* and *East* stretch up from the Lizard and along the south coast to Plymouth. These distant-sounding Celtic names, their meanings shrouded in mystery, are my chapter headings.

I have included the principal castles of Cornwall in my survey, but it would have been impossible to describe every house and garden of note. Most of the important houses are mentioned but some are discussed more summarily than others. In the case of modest manor houses and farms, I have chosen both the unusual and the typical and those of which I am fond, and I have included one fishing village, as an example of a typical Cornish small coastal community.

Further details and histories of the families who lived in these houses may be found in the appendix, referenced by page number and asterisk or other symbol.

There are also, for easy reference, a list of castles, houses and gardens that are open to the public, a map indicating the location of every place mentioned in the book, and at the end of the book an alphabetical list of every place. Every castle and house is marked on the Ordnance Survey Map of Cornwall.

The new edition has been brought up to date and includes more places and some colour photographs.

Acknowledgements

I SHOULD like to thank those owners who kindly showed me their homes and took the trouble to supply me with information about them. Their welcome and readiness to help increased the pleasure of writing this book. In particular, I should like to thank Lt. Col. Sir Arscott and Lady Molesworth-St Aubyn of Pencarrow, Mr and Mrs Michael Galsworthy of Trewithen, Mr and Mrs Peter Prideaux-Brune of Prideaux Place and Mr Robert Dorrien-Smith of Tresco Abbey for so generously providing colour illustrations and photographs. I am also grateful to the committee of the Morrab Library, Penzance for allowing me to reproduce engravings from books in its care and to Mrs Maggie Campbell-Culver, curator of Mount Edgcumbe Country Park, Mr Michael Nelhams, head gardener of Tresco Abbey Garden, Mr Tim Smit, director of Heligan Manor Gardens Project and the National Trust for their kind permission to reproduce photographs belonging to them.

Photos by Herbert Felton p.24, John Bethell p.26 (top) and p125 (foot). A Hornak p.26 (foot, Precision Ltd p.36 (top), Devon Commercial Photos p.65 (foot), Jeremy Whitaker p.79 (foot), A F Kersting pp.80, 98 (foot) & p.101 (top), Andrew Besley p.79 (foot), plates 1 (foot) & 10 (foot), E J Spear plate 6 (foot), Toby Musgrave, plate 7 (top), Michael Calderwood plate 8 (top), Tymn Lintell plates 11 (foot) & 15, and Michael Nelhams plate 16.

List of Places and Key to Map

Drawing based on John Norden's Topographical and Historical
Survey of Cornwall, 1610

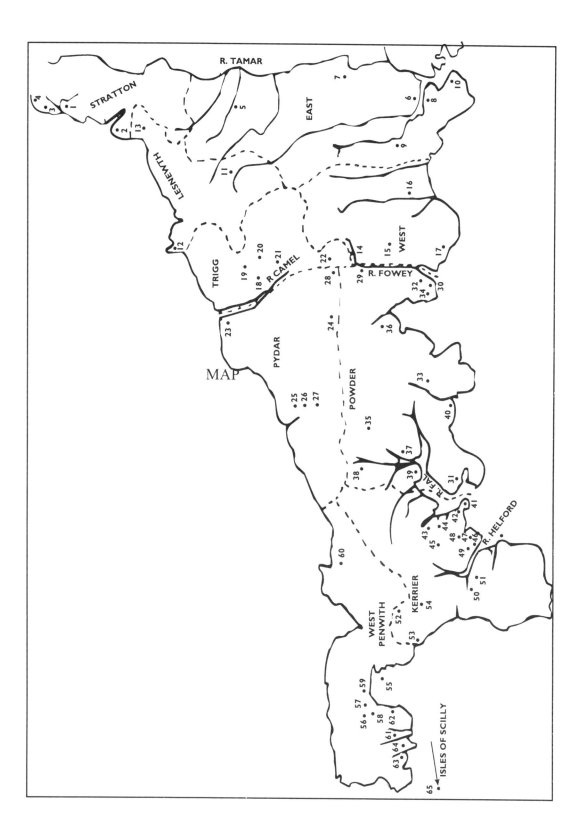

MAP

R. TAMAR

STRATTON

EAST

LESNEWTH

TRIGG

WEST

R. CAMEL

R. FOWEY

PYDAR

POWDER

R. FAL

R. HELFORD

KERRIER

WEST PENWITH

ISLES OF SCILLY

List of Castles, Houses and Gardens Open to the Public

List of Illustrations

Colour

for
Gilbert and Camilla

Introduction

CORNWALL is unlike any other British county, for the greater part of this long, south west peninsula is bounded by the Atlantic ocean. Its geography, archaeology, and climate have fashioned an independent breed of people with no great regard for their cousins across the Tamar. An understanding of Cornwall's Celtic past and dramatic history explains the modesty of some houses, the grandeur of others. The romantic inclinations of their owners are expressed in the gardens they designed and planted.

In Saxon times the Hundreds were sub-divided into manors under the jurisdiction of a local lord. William the Conqueror consolidated his conquest by strengthening this feudal system. All land ownership was vested in the king and many Saxon 'tons' became royal manors. William made his half-brother Robert, Count of Mortain, Earl of Cornwall. He gave him most of the manors in Cornwall which were held for him by Norman lords who then built castles to secure their position. Few of these French-speaking lords, many of whom held estates elsewhere, chose to reside permanently in primitive Cornwall where resources were meagre and the people spoke a language they did not understand.

In 1337 Edward III raised the earldom of Cornwall to a duchy and invested his seven-year-old son Prince Edward with the title of first Duke of Cornwall. Although the Black Prince occasionally entertained his lords and vassals and received his feudal dues, he never lived in any of his strongholds. Court influence did not exist in Cornwall. Throughout England, powerful noblemen such as the Earls of Warwick and Northumberland kept huge households, entertaining handsomely in the great halls of their castles and travelling with elaborate retinues to London in order to demonstrate their power and wealth. In Cornwall mediæval families simply cultivated their modest estates, the manors often little more than farmhouses.

With the Dissolution of the Monasteries in 1536, Cornish merchants and gentry were quick to acquire the monastic properties that came suddenly on the market. Those who supported the Reformation, enriched by the redistribution of monastic revenues and tithes, soon enlarged their old houses or built new ones. Port Eliot and Prideaux Place date from this time. A few families, the most notable being the Arundells of Lanherne, remained catholic and their estates soon fell into decay.

When relations with Catholic Spain deteriorated in the 1580s, Elizabeth I relied on the support of staunch Protestants such as Sir Richard Grenville and Sir Francis Godolphin. Although she approved unofficially of the Cornish gentry's verve in privateering and piracy against the Spaniards, she did not grace her distant and courageous subjects with a royal visit. There are no 'Prodigy' houses in Cornwall, fitted with great chambers and state apartments to receive a royal progress, but mainly unpretentious and homely Elizabethan manor houses such as Trerice, tucked out of sight in sheltered coombes.

By the end of the sixteenth century political stability and increasing prosperity led to the 'Great Rebuild'. Manor houses were enlarged, with improved heating and lighting. The yeomen modestly followed the squires' example. This spate of new building gave considerable opportunities for local craftsmen to show their skills. The huge distances and poor roads forced Cornishmen to rely on local resources. Ash-grey granite from the moors of Bodmin and Penwith was the predominant building material, durable but extremely hard to carve and not suited to fine, decorative detailing. Elvan, the Cornish name for the local quartz-porphyry, was favoured by some Georgian builders for its finer texture, ideal for ashlar masonry. Antony and Trewithen are built of the light grey Pentewan elvan brought by sea and overland from quarries near Mevagissey. Hard Cornish slate, non-porous and quick-drying, made an excellent roofing material and was quarried early on in the Fowey and Padstow areas, the great Delabole quarry being worked as early as 1600.

Richard Carew, squire of Antony and a writer of note, stresses in his *Survey of Cornwall* of 1602 that the builder's aim was to construct solid, weather-tight buildings 'seeking therethrough only strength and warmness', for they had to withstand violent storms and shut out the moisture-laden air. Throughout history Cornish architects have fought an exasperating and uphill battle against damp walls and rotting roof timbers. The search for shelter from a furious and unpredictable wind dictated the sites of domestic buildings. Consequently, the fine houses built by the gentry are hidden in deep valleys or on the banks of an estuary rather than on the exposed sea coast. For practical more than aesthetic reasons the gentry planted trees where woodland did not already exist. Farms, too, were built on sheltered inland slopes rather than on coastal hill-tops where the old Celtic fortified castles had stood. Cottages were built of cob and thatch, for timber has always been scarce in Cornwall and good quality wood was required for boat-building. The rest was used for mine props and until the advent of coal for smelting fuel.

The gentry, Carew reports in 1602, 'keep liberal, but not costly builded or furnished houses, give kind entertainment to strangers, are reverenced and beloved of their neighbours, live void of actions amongst themselves . . . They converse familiarly together and often visit one another. A gentleman and his wife will ride to make merry with his next neighbour, and after a day or twain, those two couples will go to a third, in which progress they increase like snowballs, till through their burdensome weight they break again.'

Apart from relieving the monotony of country life in this remote part of England, visited by only the most intrepid outsider, one of the main objectives of the social round was match-making. As the history of the houses unfolds, one sees how closely connected by marriage are the Cornish gentry, a kind of respectable incest winding down all the family trees. But if match-making was a career for Cornish ladies, the men led busy, active lives as landowners, magistrates, military commanders, and members of Parliament. The gentry controlled local affairs.

During the Civil War Cornwall was the scene of heavy fighting. Most of the great Cornish families were ardent royalists and Charles I rewarded many of the men who had fought for him so bravely. Some were elevated to the peerage after the Restoration and enjoyed the King's favour. The sophistication of Charles II's court gave certain families a taste for splendour and refinement. Stowe, the magnificent house of Sir John Grenville, made Earl of Bath and Baron Grenville of Kilkhampton, was considered the noblest dwelling in the West of England.

No Cornish family was rich enough to build on the scale of Blenheim Palace or influential enough to entertain government members, as Sir Robert Walpole did at Houghton Hall in Norfolk. The gentry were content to lead the lives of country squires, taking an interest in local politics, exploiting the mineral wealth found on their lands. In the latter part of the eighteenth century and well into the nineteenth, many old houses were pulled down and rebuilt with the profits from tin and copper. Architects from London such as Nash, Soane, and Wilkins were engaged to design these extravagant new houses in a variety of styles. For the first time, in a broad sense, ideas and fashions from the rest of England reached Cornwall, and with improved transport the Cornish themselves could travel further afield on excellent turnpike roads and in faster coaches.

The important houses of Cornwall are a monument to its history, for their owners helped to build it politically and economically. Modest houses, farms and cottages complete the story. Architecturally provincial and behind the times they might have been, but some of these houses, rarely mentioned in books on English country houses, form a unique chapter in the history of English architecture.

GARDENS in Cornwall, like houses, have a character of their own. Most are surrounded by woodland for protection against the wind, but a sea or river estuary can often be glimpsed through the trees. These trees may look poor specimens, stunted and misshapen, to a visitor from 'up-country' but they are cherished by their Cornish owners who have seen them do battle against the gales.

Spring comes early and the flowering season is long. Courageous snowdrops appear in January. By March daffodils cover fields and cliffs in a blanket of yellow warmth; gardens are bright with early camellias, raspberry to candy pink, and magnolias the size of water-lilies. Bluebells invade the May landscape, taking over hedgerows and meadows, a dramatic contrast to fire-red rhododendrons and azaleas. Hydrangeas bloom from August until November, their caps of blue, white, or pink lace compensating for lack of autumn colour: the wind curls and shrivels Cornish leaves before they can turn to burnished gold.

William Kent never came to this wild peninsula but his revolt against the 'artificial' in favour of a natural garden of winding paths, open vistas, and wooded glades inspired Cornish landowners to capitalise on the natural beauty of their native countryside. The sudden declivities, rocky chasms, and fallen tree trunks advocated by the Picturesque school are part of Cornwall's landscape. If the aim of the *jardin anglais* was to create an air of accident and surprise and to arouse varied sensations in the viewer, Cornwall's awesome cliffs, sublime seascapes, and exotic luxuriance contained all the drama and poetry needed to satisfy these demands.

Increasing world trade and travel brought to late eighteenth century Europe a flood of new and exciting plants. The emphasis was no longer upon design but on the creation of a flower garden. Humphry Repton, who visited north Cornwall, popularised the open terrace with surrounding flowerbeds overlooking the park, and paved the way for the plantsman's garden. Leading families in the county helped to finance the great plant collectors who journeyed to China, Asia and to North America and South America at the end of the nineteenth and beginning of the twentieth centuries. The Cornish soil, fertile, quick-draining and rich in leaf mould, was ideally suited to nurture the seeds brought back from these expeditions. Conifers, magnolias, rhododendrons, camellias, and azaleas thrive in the damp, mild atmosphere and because frost is a rarity gardeners can grow in sheltered spots out-of-doors, sub-tropical plants that must be nurtured in greenhouses in other counties. Sadly, freak hurricanes can devastate these luxuriant habitats. On January 24th-25th, 1990 storm force winds struck with terrifying force and ravaged the shelter belts in all Cornish gardens. Old plantings of Monterey pine and beech trees were virtually destroyed. Not only were trees lost, but as they fell precious shrubs were crushed beneath them or toppled themselves as the wind cut great swathes through the woodlands. Hard lessons were learned. Shelter belts are now being replanted with a mixture of tree species, including tree magnolias which, to everyone's surprise, displayed remarkable strength during the onslaught.

Cornwall is determined not only to preserve its existing garden heritage — Cornwall Gardens Trust was founded in 1988 with this objective in mind — but to play an active role in conservation in the twenty-first century. The Cornish climate offers unique opportunities to conserve vitally important Temperate Rainforest species as living Arboretum and Botanic garden collections. Rare trees, mainly conifer species, associated undershrubs, flowering herbs and ferns can be conserved by being grown in appropriate sites. The formation and scientific structuring of such collections is the work of a specialised Botanic Garden. The establishment of such a garden in Cornwall would be a valuable educational resource and the greatest possible stimulus to the long-term survival of Cornish gardens as a whole.

Cornish gardeners, however, are no mere custodians. Their success in creating new hybrids from the different species in their care, and their inventive attitude towards design make them innovators in the art and science of gardening.

1.
Stratton

Call the hind from the plough, and the herd from the fold;
Bid the wassailer cease from his revel;
And ride for old Stowe when the banner's unfurled
For the cause of King Charles and Sir Bevil.

R. S. Hawker, 'The Gate Song of Stowe'

WHEN the Saxon King Egbert invaded Devon and Cornwall in 814 he entered a Celtic and largely Christian world that knew nothing of Roman ways. Saxon domination marked the end of Cornwall's long estrangement, both geographical and cultural, from the rest of England, and the birth of a new order. The Celtic form of clan ownership of land was replaced by the Saxon feudal system, whereby the county was divided into Hundreds. Saxon influence was first felt in the north of Cornwall, and in Stratton Hundred English place names mingle with the Cornish. Often an old Celtic settlement became a Saxon manor, with the Saxon word 'ton' or 'stow' added to the Cornish name, as in Kilkhampton and Morwenstow.

After the Norman Conquest, the estates were administered by tenants-in-chief in return for military support in time of war. Many manors were held by families who had come from Normandy, the Grenvilles among them. Although they have long since left Cornwall and virtually nothing survives of their seats, their presence remains strangely alive. The countryside along the north coast between Bude and Bideford, once their territory, has changed little. A number of steep and fertile valleys, cut into the high table-land at right angles to the sea, were lovingly described by Charles Kingsley in *Westward Ho!*

Each has its upright walls, inland of rich oak-wood, nearer the sea of dark-green furze, then of smooth turf, then of weird black cliffs which range out right and left far into the deep sea, in castles, spires, and wings of jagged ironstone. Each has its narrow strip of fertile meadow, its crystal trout stream winding across and across from one foot-hill to the other; its grey stone mill, with the water sparkling and humming round the dripping wheel . . . to landward, all richness, softness and peace; to seaward, a waste and howling wilderness of rock and roller, barren to the fisherman, and hopeless to the shipwrecked mariner.

Coombe is such a valley, and on the north slope, about a mile inland from the sea, the Grenvilles chose to build their home. **Stowe** was a modest, comfortable mediæval manor house for five centuries. In 1679 it was pulled down to make way for a new, grand residence worthy of an ennobled and powerful family. Now, Stowe Barton, a handsome late-eighteenth century farmhouse standing on the hillside in solitary splendour, is the only reminder of this great seat. The sloping fields bright with yellow furze in spring, the dense woodland, the squat tower of Kilkhampton church further up the valley, are as they were centuries ago. Only the huge, glaring-white telecommunication saucers tilted upwards and outwards to sky and sea on the moorland behind are out of place as we look back at Grenville history.

From the twelfth century onwards, the Grenvilles increased their power by adding to their lands and by participating in both local and national affairs. Like most Cornish gentry, they supported the House of Lancaster and were rewarded for their loyalty after the Battle of Bosworth in 1485, when Thomas Grenville became Esquire of the Body to Henry VII. Fifty years later, in 1536, Sir Richard Grenville acquired a great deal of land upon the Dissolution of the Monasteries. As steward of Bodmin Priory's extensive property in Devon, he was in an ideal position to purchase monastic tithes as well as monastic land, the value of which was to increase dramatically later in the century.

Roger Grenville, captain of the *Mary Rose* was drowned when the ship capsized and his son, Sir Richard Grenville, also died for England, becoming a symbol of courage for generations to follow.*

Sir Richard was succeeded by his grandson, Sir Bevil, who fought in the Civil War and died in 1645. His third son, John, inherited Stowe and continued to support his sovereign.**

Charles II rewarded John handsomely for his family's devotion to the Stuart cause. In 1661 he was made Earl of Bath, Viscount Lansdowne, and Baron Grenville of Kilkhampton and Bideford. He became Lord Lieutenant of Cornwall, Lord Warden of the Stannaries (with a pension of £3,000 a year paid out of tin revenues) and Steward of the Duchy, all lucrative appointments. It was small wonder that with such riches and a privileged position at Court - he was Groom of the Stole - he decided to pull down the old house of his forefathers and build a splendid new mansion in its place.

Although the lives of the various Grenvilles are well documented, very little written material or drawings of old Stowe have come to light, and Charles Kingsley's picture of a 'huge rambling building, half castle, half dwelling-house' with the 'lofty walls of the old ballium' still standing on three sides, the southern court having become a flower garden 'with quaint terraces, statues, knots of flowers, clipped yews and hollies', is probably almost entirely imagination. Whatever its charms, John Grenville evidently did not consider old Stowe either comfortable to live in or a suitable seat for an earl. In 1679 a grand new house built of red brick in the latest classical style was erected in its place.

Surprisingly little is known about new Stowe. Celia Fiennes, who journeyed through Cornwall on horseback in 1698, bypassed Kilkhampton on her way to

Launceston and never saw Stowe, although she knew it had 'fine stables of horses and gardens'. A contemporary drawing has survived, showing an impressive single block of four storeys with two projecting wings on either side. The roof is hipped, with dormer windows to light the top attic storey, while a grand staircase in the centre leads up to the ground floor. Its design resembles that of Clarendon House, Piccadilly, built for the great Lord Chancellor, Edward Hyde, by Roger Pratt in 1664, or Belton House in Lincolnshire, built twenty years later. Stowe was in the forefront of fashion and stylishness, massive yet serene with its straight elegant lines and symmetrical disposition. Its architect is not known but was undoubtedly a disciple of Inigo Jones and Roger Pratt. Such a sophisticated design - and on such a scale - together with the lavish use of building materials foreign to the county, were unknown in Cornwall at this time and suggest an outsider's hand. The magnificence of Stowe was unrivalled in the West of England.

Ironically, great Stowe's history is a short and sad one. John Grenville died in 1701, having enjoyed the house for twenty years, but henceforth personal tragedy brought about Stowe's demise. John's eldest son Charles shot himself accidentally while preparing to go to his father's funeral and was buried with him in Kilkhampton church. His small son Henry succeeded him as 3rd Earl of Bath but died of smallpox in 1711. A bitter family quarrel ensued, Jane and Grace Grenville, the 1st Earl's daughters, contesting the claim to the estates by their cousin George Granville. In the end, after much legal wrangling, George renounced his claim. Grace took over the Cornish estates and Jane those in Devon. Grace, created Countess Granville in her own right, briefly inhabited Stowe, but she married a Carteret whose seat was in Jersey. The mechanics of looking after her Cornish mansion became increasingly irksome. The expense was considerable and Stowe, for all its grandeur, was perishingly cold in winter. It must have been a hard decision to take, but in 1739 - just sixty years after its erection - she had it demolished.

Virtually nothing survives. The bricks and masonry, as well as fine panelling and plasterwork inside, were quickly taken and were incorporated into houses both in the area and further afield. The late seventeenth-century panelling and Grinling Gibbons-style carvings in the Grenville Room at Prideaux Place, Padstow, together with a painting of *The Rape of Europa* by Antonio Verrio above the chimney-piece, are traditionally held to have come from Stowe. The porch is now part of the town hall of South Molton in Devon.

Today a visitor looking at **Stowe Barton**, which has been erected on the site of the stables, may conjure up a vision of the great house with its proud cupola looking over the sea. The high walls of an oblong carriage-wash in front of the stables still stand and can be seen on the side of the road just below the farmhouse. Carriages gleaming in the sun can be imagined clattering through the entrance gate, past formally laid-out walled gardens with fountains and parterres,

Stowe. View of Stowe from Coombe valley. Drawn by Edmund Prideaux in the 1730s.

Stowe. A drawing by Edmund Prideaux made shortly before the house was demolished in 1739.

and up to the grand east front. Here visitors would alight, admiring the prospect over the valley towards Kilkhampton before ascending the elegant steps to the entrance hall. The coachmen would then have made their way round to the coach house by the west front.

THE Arundell family has left its mark in Stratton Hundred. **Ebbingford Manor**, outside Bude, was added to their estates in 1433, when Joan Durrant married an Arundell. For more than a century Ebbingford was one of the main Arundell residences. The 3rd Sir John Arundell died in 1561, probably at Ebbingford, and is buried with other Arundells in nearby Stratton church. His second son John set about rebuilding Trerice, the family seat near Newquay. He inherited considerable wealth from his father and married an heiress, Katherine Coswarth, from the adjoining parish. After Katherine's death he married Gertrude Dennys of Holcombe, and it was possibly she who enlarged Ebbingford.

Originally Ebbingford consisted of a hall rising to the roof with, on the right-hand side, a bedchamber on the first floor and dining-room below. Separate buildings contained stables and kitchens. Gertrude added the stable block to the left of the hall, which was divided from the house by a slype or passageway. This block was subsequently converted into a chapel. The square, mullioned granite windows and huge chimney-stacks also date from Gertrude's time. After her death the newly-built Trerice presumably became the favourite Arundell residence, although Ebbbingford was a useful outlet for their numerous children.

Richard Carew, who married Katherine Arundell's daughter Juliana, paints an attractive picture of Ebbingford in his *Survey of Cornwall*.

Master Arundell of Trerice possesseth a pleasant seated house and domain called Efford alias Ebbingford and that not unproperly because every low water there affordeth passage to the other shore; but now it may take a new name for his better plight for this gentleman hath, to his great charges builded a salt-water mill athwart this bay, whose causeway serveth as a very convenient bridge to save the wayfarer's former trouble, let, and danger.

The salt water mill can still be seen by the side of Nanny Moore's Bridge in Bude. A large stone set in one corner bears the characters AJA 1589, for Anne and John Arundell.

In 1643 Ebbingford was occupied by Mary Arundell, the eldest daughter of the 5th Sir John. Her younger sister Anna had married Colonel John Trevanion, a troop commander in Sir Bevil Grenville's army. Trevanion and his soldiers camped at Ebbingford on the night of May 15th, 1643 before the battle of Stamford Hill near Stratton. Much merry-making eased the tension as tactics were discussed on the eve of the battle. Perhaps this was the last night that he and Anna spent together. Trevanion's victory at Stratton was short-lived, for he

Stowe Barton (late 18th century) erected on the site of the stables at Stowe. The walls of the old carriage wash can be seen by the roadside.

Ebbingford Manor, Bude. The façade has 16th century mullioned windows (to the left of the porch) and Georgian sash windows (to the right).

died, as Sir Bevil did, at Lansdowne that July.

After the Restoration very little is heard of Ebbingford. The newly created Baron Arundell of Trerice presumably let it to tenant farmers. When, in 1768, the 4th Baron died without issue, the Arundell estates passed to his wife's nephew, William Wentworth of Henbury in Dorset. A complicated settlement decreed that if William's son and daughter were to die without children the estates should go to the Aclands of Killerton, descendants of Margaret Acland, wife of the 2nd Baron of Arundell. This in fact happened and in 1802 Ebbingford, like Trerice, became the property of Sir Thomas Dyke-Acland. The Aclands never lived at Ebbingford, for part of it was already let to a Colonel Wrey I'ans. By this time Georgian sash windows had been put in and two brick chimney-stacks added. The other part of the house was a farm and tradition has it that the first Methodist services in Bude were held in it in the 1820s.

In 1861 the Aclands gave Ebbingford to the Church Commissioners for use as a vicarage. It remained so until 1953, when the current vicar and the father of the present owner agreed to swop houses. Canon Walter Prest moved to 8 Falcon Terrace and Sir Dudley Stamp came to Ebbingford. It is truly remarkable that in 800 years Ebbingford has never been offered for sale on the open market. The walled garden shuts out the hurly-burly of Bude itself and embraces the house, as if to protect it from the ravages of time.

A FEW miles north of Stowe lies the village of Morwenstow, with its church, glebe farm, and vicarage. **Morwenstow Vicarage** was built in 1837 by Robert Stephen Hawker, the eccentric vicar of the parish who is remembered both for his poems and for his curious behaviour. Morwenstow is bleak and windswept. The cliffs nearby rise to almost four hundred feet and were notorious as a death trap for sailors. Hawker noticed that his sheep always used to shelter from storms on the ground immediately below the church, and so chose this site for his vicarage. A practical man who saw no need to employ an architect, he consulted T. F. Hunt's *Designs for Parsonage Houses* and adapted a model for 'a Clergyman's house on a moderate scale'. A solid, gabled Victorian gothic house, its chimneys are its most interesting feature. They were all built to look like the church towers in parishes in which Hawker had previously lived - Stratton, Whitstone, North Tamerton, and Oxford. The kitchen chimney resembles his mother's tomb. Over the front door is a verse inscribed in stone:

A House, a Glebe, a Pound a Day,
A Pleasant Place to Watch and Pray
Be true to Church - Be kind to poor,
O Minister, for ever more.

It is not a particularly attractive house, but some knowledge of Hawker and

Morwenstow churchyard, just above the vicarage, with the white-painted figurehead of the wrecked Caledonia to the left.

Morwenstow Vicarage, built by R. S. Hawker in 1837.

his parish adds much to its interest. In 1823 he married Charlotte I'ans, third daughter of Colonel Wrey I'ans of Ebbingford, where no doubt the proposal took place. Although she was forty-one and he was nineteen, they were devoted to one another and she performed her duties as a vicar's wife extremely well. Hawker described her face as 'a perfect image of noble Womanhood - oval - blue-eyed - with a nose slightly curved somewhat like my own - a firm mouth, and a forehead moderately high banded with soft light hair that never turned grey to the last'. She played the piano, was fond of literature, and above all, did not mind the isolation of this 'godforsaken' parish.

In 1864 Hawker wrote 'Mine is without exception the most desolate parish for food in the country. We have no parish butcher - I remember when there were three - no carrier or coach, not even a shop.' Morwenstow folk had to grow their own produce and buy the occasional extras from travelling pedlars. Hawker's eight hundred or so parishioners were mainly farm labourers, uneducated and pitifully poor. 'How they exist is a mystery,' comments Hawker, 'especially after the potato blight.' The agricultural wage was eight shillings a week, hardly enough for rent, fuel, and clothing, after paying for their frugal diet of bread, potatoes, garlic and tea.

Hawker was a compassionate man and his letters are full of details about the appalling housing conditions in his parish. Most families lived in one room, which was damp, dirty, and devoid of sanitation. Open cesspools were the norm. Typhus and cholera were common and child mortality high. The villagers searched the beaches for wreckage in the hope of finding something that would help to relieve their dismal existence.*

Hawker was prone to melancholia and however much he busied himself with parish affairs felt miserable and lonely after Charlotte's death. In 1864 he married Pauline Kuczynski, a half-English, half-Polish woman of twenty, forty years his junior. He met her when a Yorkshire vicar brought his family to Morwenstow to convalesce. Pauline came with them as nursery governess to the children. She and Hawker were devoted to one another and she bore him three daughters before he died in 1875.

MORWENSTOW is hardly a village in the accepted sense, since there are no houses round the church save for the vicarage and farm. A mile to the north, however, just south of Marsland stream which runs into the Atlantic and marks the Cornwall-Devon boundary, is the **Manor of Marsland**. Built of the local rubblestone in the late sixteenth or early seventeenth century, it forms four sides of a square. A hall, parlour, cellar, front and back kitchens, and a salting house (for the salting down of meat) are grouped round the court. On the gable above the salting house are the initials W. A. and the date 1656 carved on a stone. This part of the house was rebuilt in the mid-seventeenth century when modernisation was deemed necessary. A fine new bedchamber was made in the upper storey, the

Marsland Manor. The gatehouse.

Marsland Manor. The mid-17th century court.

date 1662 being visible in the plaster.

A small gatehouse forms one side of the court, a reminder that the concept of fortification had not yet disappeared in this remote corner of England. A narrow entrance way would keep intruders out.

In Kingsley's *Westward Ho!*, Henry Davils of Marsland taught Amyas Leigh 'how to catch trout when he was staying down at Stowe'; another friend, Will Cary, galloped off to Marsland Mouth to round up two Jesuit priests for Sir Richard Grenville. Perhaps this tiny manor was their home.

2.
East

This triple-crowned mounte, though abandoned,
retayneth the forme, but not the fortune and favour
of former times.

John Norden, *Description of Cornwall*, 1610

THE year after William I's victory over King Harold at Hastings, the Norman army was sent to quell a rising in Exeter. After a brief siege, the Normans marched further west, across the river Tamar, which forms the eastern boundary of East Hundred and of Cornwall itself. The 1st Earl of Cornwall chose Launceston (or Dunheved as it is called in Domesday Book) as the administrative centre of his domain. The simple earth and timber castle he built on the summit of the hill gave him a superb vantage point. No hostile force could approach from Bodmin moor to the west or from Dartmoor to the east without being detected.

Although by the end of the twelfth century military architects felt that the fortification of a larger area by means of a massive curtain wall with several entrances provided a more flexible type of defence, giving room to launch a counter-attack, **Launceston Castle** did not follow this trend. Surprisingly, given the strategic importance of the site, no further building took place until well into the thirteenth century when Richard, younger brother of Henry III, became Earl of Cornwall in 1227.

Richard modernised the castle, which he made his headquarters, and built most of the stonework we see today. He constructed a shell keep on the motte or mound, replacing the earlier wooden palisade with a circular stone wall. Lean-to buildings were constructed round it on the outside, to provide basic accommodation on the mound, while behind the wall, within the keep itself, the soldier now had a safe platform from which to fight. At a later date a round tower rising one storey higher was built inside the shell keep, the narrow passage between the two being roofed over at wall-walk level. This increased the width of the wall-walk and meant the ground floor premises were better protected. The joist holes for this roof can be seen half-way up the tower. The wall-walk survives in part, although the parapet has almost gone, and one can see in the thickness of the wall the remains of the two staircases which led up to it. On the west side of the keep is a large recess which contained one or two *garderobes* or privies which were ingeniously flushed out in wet weather by the drain from the wall-walk.

The tower, built of a dark-coloured shale, is entered by a pointed arch doorway on the west side. The ground-floor room has no windows and was presumably used for storage. A staircase leads up to the first-floor room which is well lit by a pointed window. There is also a fireplace with the remains of a slightly projecting hood corbelled out from the wall.

Access to the shell keep was strongly defended. A roofed-over staircase with high walls on either side and a gatehouse at the foot led up the precipitous south side of the motte. To reach this bottom gatehouse an intruder would first have had to cross the moat that protected the south and east sides of the castle, and break through the massive south gate, now the main entrance to the castle from the town. Within this gate lies the bailey of the castle, known as Castle Green ever since it was turned into a landscaped park in Victorian times. The west side of the bailey was protected by a steep slope and curtain wall, part of which still survives to the west of the south gate.

The Black Prince's survey of the castle, made in 1337 and the earliest surviving documentary evidence of the stone structures, makes it quite clear that the buildings within the bailey were the domestic and administrative quarters of the castle. There were three separate halls. The largest was the assize hall, where petitions were presented and feudal dues paid. Here, wrong-doers were punished and flung into the nearby gaols. This hall was still used 'for syses and sessions' when John Leland, Henry VIII's librarian, visited Launceston in 1539, and was better maintained than the other buildings because of its legal function.

The second hall with walls 'of timber and plank', together with a chamber and small chapel, formed a suite of rooms for the use of the Earl. Because the Earls of Cornwall so rarely came to Launceston, these fell quickly into disrepair, and had disappeared by Leland's time. Earl Richard is supposed to have spent Christmas here, shortly before his coronation as Holy Roman Emperor at Aachen in 1257 and to have raised troops in Launceston for the battle of Lewes in 1264. After his death in 1272, the Earl's quarters lay empty for a long time. The third and smallest hall 'convenient for the Constable', with a chamber and cellar, survived until the seventeenth century.

Two prisons are mentioned in the 1337 survey, one of which may be the small dank room opening off the north gate, later known as the Doomsdale Tower. The Quaker, George Fox, was imprisoned here in 1656 for refusing to take off his hat to the judge and pay the fines for the illegal distribution of religious tracts. He and his two companions also refused to pay their gaoler the outrageous sum of seven shillings a week for food and were kept in the filthy Doomsdale Tower for five months for daring to protest against such extortion. A modern plaque commemorating their bravery was placed above the doorway in the north gate by the Society of Friends. Fox was not the only prisoner to have suffered for his faith. Many Catholic recusants including Francis Tregian were imprisoned at Launceston in the latter part of the sixteenth century for their adherence to the Church of Rome.

The remains of the kitchens, ovens, pantry, and brewhouse can be seen to the west of Castle Green. The deer park which once supplied venison for the Earl's table, as well as timber for repair work, has disappeared. By the mid-fourteenth century the whole castle complex was in dire need of repair. Pigs had trampled down the moat and weakened the stone foundations, but neglect and lack of funds to carry out the necessary renovations were the chief cause of decay.

Launceston held out for the King during the Civil War, finally surrendering to Fairfax's army on February 25th, 1646, but by then the only habitable part of the castle was the gatehouse, possibly the south gate containing two rooms in which the constable lived. The castle never again performed a military role. It was so near to collapse that the Parliamentarians did not bother to demolish it, as they did Pontefract Castle in Yorkshire, in accordance with their general policy. When the assizes and county gaol were moved to Bodmin in the 1840s, Launceston Castle ceased to be the centre of Cornwall's legal administration.

THE Normans built another fortress near Saltash. They had to be able to repel raiders coming up the Tamar from Plymouth Sound, and **Trematon Castle**, standing two hundred feet above Forder creek on the north bank of the Lynher, commands extensive views up and down stream. Domesday Book records that a Norman lord, Reginald de Valletort, held Trematon Castle, together with thirty-three manors forming the 'honour' of Trematon, for Robert of Mortain. The Valletort family remained in control of these lands until 1270 when Richard, Earl of Cornwall, consolidated his position by adding Trematon to his other Cornish strongholds.

The site of Trematon Castle - the name comes from the Cornish *tre* (homestead, town) and *matern* (king's) - may well have been known to the Romans and Saxons. Pieces of pre-Norman carved stone have been found within the castle precincts, suggesting the existence of an early encampment. The building of the present castle was begun by Robert of Mortain in 1080 and completed in the mid-thirteenth century. It is of the same 'motte and bailey' design as Launceston. The motte, an artificially raised mound built on existing rock, supports the oval shell keep built by Richard, Earl of Cornwall. Its walls are thirty feet high and ten feet thick. Nothing remains of the buildings inside the keep, but holes for the beams and stone supports for the roof timbers or vaultings bear witness to the Earl's private quarters which consisted of a hall, lodging chamber, and kitchen.

A large part of the protective curtain wall stretching out from the keep still stands. This once surrounded the entire bailey and formed a triangular-shaped courtyard of almost an acre. Stables, quarters for the Earl's retinue, kitchens, a hall and a chapel were built within this enclosure. A fine, square gatehouse built by Edmund, Earl of Cornwall, towards the end of the thirteenth century has also survived. At ground level there are dungeons and rooms with slits in the walls

Launceston Castle (mid-13th century). The shell keep and gatehouse.

Trematon Castle. View from the river Lynher, from Lysons' *Magna Britannica.*

for bowmen, as well as two portcullises. The accommodation was up to date and luxurious. Each room has a stone fireplace comprising two slim columns with foliated capitals on either side of a hooded lintel. The mason's desire to make the fireplace decorative as well as functional suggests the presence of a royal visitor. The Black Prince occasionally came to Trematon and would have lodged here rather than in the primitive quarters inside the keep.

In 1549 Trematon Castle was attacked by Humphry Arundell, leader of those Cornishmen who objected to the first Book of Common Prayer introduced in Edward VI's Act of Uniformity. This forbade the use of Latin and the saying of Mass. Richard Grenville, a staunch supporter of the Crown, was forced to withdraw to Trematon, ready to withstand a siege. His lily-livered men, however, clambered over the castle walls at dead of night and made their escape. Alone and unarmed, Grenville met the rebels at the small sally gate which still stands. One honourable soldier was no match for Arundell's unscrupulous troops and, as Carew reported some fifty years later, 'those rake-hels stepped between him and home, laid hold on his aged and unweyldie body and threatened to leave it lifeless if the enclosed did not wave their resistance'. The seventy-year-old veteran was ignominiously carted off to Launceston gaol while Trematon was ransacked. Women 'were stripped from their apparel to their very smocks and some of their fingers broken to pluck away their rings'.

In 1580 Sir Francis Drake is said to have stored a huge amount of silver at Trematon. This treasure had been seized from Spanish ships during Drake's sea voyages and needed a secure resting-place until it was either shipped or trundled in wagons to the Tower of London. By now, the castle had, generally speaking, outlived its usefulness. Twenty years later, Carew noted in his *Survey of Cornwall* that 'all the inner buildings falleth daily into ruin and decay only there remains the ivy tappised walls and a good dwelling for the keeper and his gaol'. Neither Roundheads nor Cavaliers made use of Trematon during the Civil War. It was beyond repair.

The ultimate fate of the castle precincts is an unusual and happy one. In 1807 Benjamin Tucker, a naval man who was appointed Surveyor General to the Duchy of Cornwall, secured a ninety-year lease on the castle from the Prince Regent, part of the agreement being that he would spend £1,000 on the building of a house within the inner bailey walls. It is not known whom Tucker chose as his architect, but whoever it was proved sensitive to the romantic qualities of the site. He built a simple, rectangular Regency villa whose elegant, straight lines and smooth stuccoed walls - now a delicate soft beige colour - are the perfect foil to the round, roughly-hewn stone walls of the castle keep which towers to one side of it. Windows along one side of the house look out at the old castellated curtain wall leading up to the keep. Today a well-stocked herbaceous border runs its length and a lawn slopes down to the gravel sweep in front of the porch. The other façade faces Edmund's gatehouse, its verticality an effective contrast to the

Trematon Castle.
The late 13th-century
gatehouse.

The Regency Villa
within the inner
bailey walls of
Trematon Castle.

long, low proportions of the villa. Tucker pulled down a section of curtain wall on either side of the gatehouse because it blocked out the potentially superb view. Now, in the distance, you can see the wooded slopes of Antony on the other side of the Lynher and watch ships move slowly past.

In 1846 Queen Victoria was cruising with Prince Albert in the Royal Yacht *Victoria and Albert*. They took a boat trip up the Tamar in the yacht's tender *Fairy*, and scores of onlookers lined the river bank in the hope of catching a glimpse of their sovereign. When she saw Trematon high up on its mound she noted with satisfaction 'that it all belonged to Bertie as Duke of Cornwall'. Trematon still belongs to the Duchy and, like Tucker before them, the present owners are lessees. They are enthusiastic tenants who have put their hearts into the upkeep of both house and garden. The latter is full of surprises. An orchard of apple and pear trees leads into an Italian garden with romantic-looking sculptures placed incongruously in the grass or next to a crumbling mediæval wall. The steepness of the paths, either up to the keep or down to the picturesque creek and village of Forder, reminds us of the impregnability of Trematon and its former military role; the gravel walks and flowerbeds are proof of Trematon's domestic *raison d'être* today.

The river Tamar, a natural boundary between Devon and Cornwall, was not merely important from a military standpoint. Before the advent of the railway it provided the main mode of transport for everything this part of Cornwall needed. The roads were much used by trains of pack animals and were frequently impassable in wet weather. Sheet maps of Cornwall were neither accurate nor detailed, and since sign-posts were scarce the chance of taking a wrong turn in the tangle of high-hedged lanes was high. The river, which twists through the countryside like a benevolent snake, was a more reliable highway.

The numerous quays along its banks were served by sailing barges which were able to tack up and down river. Coal and limestone were brought up river from Plymouth to feed the lime-kilns on these quays, lime being needed to fertilise the arable land upon which the economy of every estate depended. The agricultural produce of the farms and market gardens was sent down river cheaply and efficiently. The Tamar also offered the Cornishman relatively easy access, by boat to Plymouth, to the rest of England. Journeys by river and sea were quicker and safer than those made by road.

Quite apart from the practicality of living close to the river, the wooded valleys provided shelter from cold winds as well as picturesque views across the water. Some of the loveliest and largest houses in Cornwall are built on the banks of the Tamar.

Cotehele, the most important Tudor house in the county that now belongs to the National Trust, stands high above the river near Calstock. The maze of lanes that criss-cross the rolling fields do not lead to a grand approach. You stumble upon Cotehele by chance. Its granite walls are hidden from sight among trees, its semi-fortified appearance bidding the stranger keep his distance.

The house takes its name from Hilaria de Cotehele who married a Devonian, William Edgcumbe, in 1353. William and his descendants lived at Cotehele for the next two hundred years, by which time the Edgcumbes had become one of the leading families in Cornwall. Hilaria's house was a small neat square. The rough sandstone rubble walls and round-headed lancets on either side of the gatehouse in the middle of the south wing probably date from her time. It was not until the end of the fourteenth century that extensive alterations were made.

After an eventful life the 1st Sir Richard Edgcumbe retired to Cotehele where he lived until his death in 1489. He built the buttressed barn and present granite gatehouse in the conventional Gothic manner, with a pointed arch entrance and castellated parapet round the top. He was also responsible for the upper floor round the inner Hall Court and for a new chapel with a bellcote and finials of moulded granite in a corner of the Retainers' Court. Here, the two-light pointed windows beneath square dripcourses also date from Sir Richard's time. The imposing pointed archway into the Hall Court, with a porter's squint in the wall on the left of it, is thought to have been the main entrance in Hilaria's day, since traces of a road leading to it have been found beneath the meadows.*

Sir Richard redesigned the approach from the south side. Under the gatehouse a narrow cobbled passage, wide enough for a pack horse, leads into the Hall Court. This court was completed by Sir Richard's son Piers, who had married an heiress called Joan Durnford. She owned a considerable amount of land on both sides of the Tamar, so Piers Edgcumbe could easily afford to complete his father's proposed scheme for the enlargement of Cotehele. Building continued until his death in 1539, the great hall which one enters from the hall court being his major contribution.

One of the present delights of Cotehele is that the original house and contents have been preserved virtually intact. In 1553 Sir Pier's son Richard built a house in the park at Mount Edgcumbe on Plymouth Sound, part of his mother's Rame Head property. This became the Edgcumbe family's main seat. Henceforth Cotehele was only occupied spasmodically, the ideal retreat for widows or elderly relatives. No further additions were made except for the north-west tower in 1627. This was still castellated in the Gothic tradition, but its windows are square-headed. Apart from the east front, which was reconstituted for a widowed Countess of Edgcumbe in 1862, the rest of Cotehele, including the furnishings, has remained undisturbed. Much of the furniture is exactly as it was when stiff-ruffed ladies and gentlemen walked through the rooms chattering, laughing or complaining of the cold.

The design of Sir Piers Edgcumbe's great hall, which contrary to mediæval tradition has no screens passage, illustrates how behind-the-times Cornish builders often were. Hammerbeam roofs had evolved in the fourteenth century, the most

Photo, Herbert Felton. By kind permission of the National Trust.

Cotehele. The Retainers' Court, showing the archway and porter's squint leading to the Hall Court, probab the original mediæval entrance to Cotehele.

Cotehele. The Hall Court, showing the exterior of the hall c. 1520, with the wide arch leading to the Chape and Retainers' Court c. 1480 on the west wall.

Photo, Herbert Felton. By kind permission of the National Trust.

famous example being that of Westminster Hall (1397-9), and although most commonly found in East Anglia, became popular elsewhere. Henry VIII favoured a hammerbeam roof when he built the great hall at Hampton Court in the 1530s. But at Cotehele, which was built only a decade earlier, the roof is of a type fashionable in the fourteenth century, the great hall of Penshurst Place in Kent (1341-8) being similar in appearance. The slope of the roof is divided by three horizontal beams or purlins which are strengthened by moulded arched supports. These windbraces interlock to form a uniform pattern which rises in four tiers. The absence of any tie-beams adds to the feeling of height. A neighbour, Henry Trecarrel, used the same technique for the hall of his manor house, Trecarrel, now the barn of a farm a few miles south of Launceston.

The surprisingly small kitchen at Cotehele is contemporary with the hall and full of interesting equipment.. The flour ground in the estate mill (which can be visited) was stored in a covered wooden hutch; butter and salted meats were kept in pottery crocks, while a huge pestle and mortar was used for pounding meat and herbs, as well as for breaking up blocks of salt and sugar. Pot-hooks with adjustable hangers for the various cooking vessels hang in the huge hearth. On a wintry day the fires in the hall and kitchen are lit and it is easy to imagine the cook keeping an eye on the heavy pots over the hearth or putting her feet up on the settle when her work was done. The ovens in the middle of the wall were used for baking bread, cakes, and pies. A fire of dry sticks or furze would be lit and the red hot embers raked out when the oven was sufficiently heated. The dough would then be pushed into the oven with a long wooden peel or flat shovel, and the door sealed with clay.

Cotehele is particularly rich in textiles. The plastered walls of most of the rooms are hung from cornice to dado with seventeenth or early eighteenth century Flemish and English tapestries. These colourful alternatives to wood panelling helped to shut out the draughts. They were cut to fit the walls and often adjacent panels did not match in terms of subject matter. In the White Bedroom, for example, there are three Mortlake tapestries depicting mythological scenes, two Flemish panels showing a crowing cockerel and figures in armour, and another English fragment illustrating a maritime scene.

All the needlework at Cotehele is in a remarkable state of preservation because wear and tear from the seventeenth century onwards was minimal. The walnut four-poster bed in the White Bedroom is hung with typical Jacobean crewel embroidery, soft blue, musky pink and green stylised flowers and trees in wool being mounted on linen. The crewelwork curtains, similar to those on the famous Abigail Pett bed in the Victoria and Albert Museum, depict a lively hunting scene with deer and hounds on the lower border. The bed hangings in the South Room - the solar of the Tudor house with a squint looking down into the hall — are of red wool worked in stem stitch, back stitch and coral knot mounted on linen. Lilies and oak leaves form the basis of the pattern. There are

Cotehele. The Hall.

Photo, John Bethell. By kind permission of the National Trust.

Cotehele. The kitchen, showing the oven and a huge pestle and mortar.

Photo, A Hornak. By kind permission of the National Trust.

also superb examples of seventeenth century *gros point* embroidery as well as silk hangings and canopies.

If time seems to have stopped inside the house, the garden shows more recent activity. Much of the planting was done in late Victorian times. In the north-west corner of the house is the meadow, approached through an archway in the Retainers' Court. Nineteenth-century prints show cows being milked here; now it is planted with a mass of daffodils. Nearby is the upper garden, surrounded by a mediæval wall covered with jasmine and forsythia. Fuchsias and peonies, regal purple and shocking pink, flank the path beside a water-lily pond and on the lawn below are a magnificent tulip tree and golden ash.

A path leads past the Jacobean tower and round the side of the house to the east front. You pass a group of white thorn and whitebeam trees, an old Judas tree, a mulberry, a cork oak, and a silver weeping lime, as well as fiery rhododendrons and milky white wisteria. On the three terraces that descend in steps below the east front purple polyanthus flower in spring, scarlet roses in summer. Two huge magnolias spread their branches over more steps leading down to the valley garden. It is worthwhile pausing here to admire the view. Crimson rhododendrons and deep pink camellias overhang a thatched Victorian summerhouse in front of a mediæval pond; beyond is the old dovecote.

The lower part of the valley, full of birdsong, is planted with spindly spruce and larches but also contains rarer specimens such as *Davidia involucrata* (known as the Dove Tree because of its large white bracts which hang in pairs), and *Gunnera manicata* which resembles a gigantic rhubarb plant. All these trees and shrubs protect the garden from east winds.

Communications were so bad in Tudor times that the estate had to be more or less self-sufficient. The buildings clustered round the quay, which was abandoned at the turn of the century, are a unique reminder of industrial activity at Cotehele. The National Trust has dug out and repaired the little docks and restored the warehouses, one of which has been turned into a small museum explaining the river economy. Half a mile up a stream that runs into the Tamar just below the quay is the manor mill, where corn was ground to provide flour for the house. This has been restored and is once again in working order, like the horse-powered cider mill beside it. Outbuildings nearby contain the blacksmith's forge and the wheelwright's and saddler's shops. You can even see the sawpit where wood was sawn into planks ready for the carpenter.

COTEHELE is such a haven of peace and beauty that it is hard to appreciate why the Edgcumbes decided to live at **Mount Edgcumbe**. They could not have chosen a more different site. Whereas Cotehele is protected by woods and is invisible to the outside world, Mount Edgcumbe is as vulnerable as it could be, standing open and exposed on a hill overlooking Plymouth Sound. Perhaps the Edgcumbes were tired of being hemmed in, and relished the thought of unlimited space, magnificent sea views, a larger, more modern house and, if Cotehele was too inaccessible in bad weather, a nearby town.

Piers Edgcumbe's son, Richard, came into a substantial inheritance on the death of his father in 1539, and eight years later began to build a mansion in the enclosed deer park. A local mason called Roger Palmer from North Buckland built him an oblong house which was still mediæval in appearance since the front was not fully symmetrical. It had round, battlemented towers at each corner and a magnificent hall lit from the top by clerestory windows. This huge room invited the admiration of all who saw it. Richard's grandson, Richard Carew, writing in 1600, describes how this hall 'rising in the midst above the rest, yieldeth a stately sound as you enter the same. In summer, the opened casements admit refreshing coolness, in winter, the two closed doors exclude all offensive coldness.' The height and light of such a room probably thrilled the Edgcumbes after the dark, low-ceilinged rooms at Cotehele.

From the parlour and dining-room they could look across the Sound towards Plymouth or watch the boats sailing up the Tamar towards Saltash. Rich meadows and fertile arable land 'abundantly answereth a housekeepers necessities', Carew goes on, while 'a little below the house, in the summer evenings, sein boats come in and draw with their nets for fish, whither the gentry of the house walking down, take the pleasure of the sight, and sometimes, at all adventures, buy the profit of the draughts'. The admirals of the Spanish and Dutch fleets whom Sir Richard entertained in Queen Mary's reign must have told their countrymen of the splendours of Mount Edgcumbe, for forty years later the Spanish Duke of Medina Sidonia was apparently determined to live there once the Armada had conquered Britain.

In the early nineteenth century Mount Edgcumbe was a well-known beauty spot which visitors from all over England came to admire.

Tragically, those very qualities that made Mount Edgcumbe such an agreeable dwelling-place — its hilltop position and proximity to a sea port — were the cause of its destruction. It was gutted by a German incendiary bomb in April 1941, during a particularly heavy raid on Plymouth, and a large part of the contents, including a number of portraits by Reynolds which hung in the dining-room, went up in flames.

A rebuilding programme was launched in 1958, but compensation was not sufficient to allow a reconstruction of the eighteenth century west wing. The Mount Edgcumbe of today resembles the original, smaller sixteenth century edifice. The sturdy outer walls and octagonal towers (which replaced the original round towers in the eighteenth century) managed to withstand the bombardment and were quickly repaired but the interior had to be entirely rebuilt. The hall is still centrally placed and lit from above, but an elegant main staircase now leads from it to a gallery at first-floor level. The cornices, doorheads, and chimney-pieces of the principal reception rooms on the ground floor are of such superb

A view of Mount Edgcumbe
House from Plymouth Sound,
drawn by Edmund Prideaux
in the 1730s.

Mount Edcumbe House showing
one of its octagonal towers.

craftsmanship that it is easy to believe they are late Georgian in the company of the fine eighteenth-century furniture which survived the onslaught.

By 1789, when George Edgcumbe became the first Earl of Mount Edgcumbe, the formal lower garden by the water's edge and the long avenue from the ferry up to the house had all but disappeared, George's brother, the previous Lord Edgcumbe, having abandoned formality for a more naturalistic, picturesque lay-out. In the 1750s he built a ruin overlooking the sea with a tower and an authentic-looking gothic window, not to mention plenty of ivy, moss, and lichen on its walls. Zig-zag walks were laid out nearby and a vast park was planted with the trees that we see today. George Edgcumbe and his son, Lord Valletort, continued the romanticising process and were responsible for the final plan of the park and gardens, which have scarcely altered since.

Uvedale Price, whose *Essay on the Picturesque* (1794) radically affected nineteenth-century English garden design, thought Mount Edgcumbe was a 'wonderful place'. Detesting the monotonous 'clumping and belting' of trees in Capability Brown's artificially-created landscaped parks, Price praised the natural grandeur of Mount Edgcumbe with its spectacular setting, impressive views and sudden contrasts. Seats and buildings including follies were positioned throughout the park not only to introduce different associations to the mind but to allow the visitor to pause and enjoy each successive vista. Fanny Burney experienced the delight and excitement of these sudden contrasts, when she visited Mount Edgcumbe in 1789 as maid of honour to Queen Caroline. 'In one moment you might suppose yourself cast on a desert island, and the next find yourself in the most fertile and luxuriant country'.

A guide-book published in the 1820s entitled *A Walk Around Mount Edgcumbe* takes the visitor on a tour of the grounds. It is still possible to identify most of the attractions described. The tour begins in the upper park on the high ground to the south of the house and follows the main drive as it twists through the woods and along the coast. The first section was known as the Great Terrace, high above the sea, the next Picklecombe, 'a little valley so regularly scooped out by nature as almost to bear the appearance of art'. Further on, an evergreen plantation led to a stone arch 'like a perforation of the natural rock' and into a number of walks snaking up and down the hillside. Plenty of benches were provided for the visitor to sit and marvel at the views. The trees are now thicker and taller here so that some of the vistas have vanished, and the zig-zag walks have almost gone. The drive continued through more woods to emerge into an open park with the gothic ruin as one of its focal points.

If the park and woods, with their dark dells and hidden glades, provoked gloomy, awesome thoughts, the adjacent pleasure gardens brought nothing but delight. An Ionic rotunda on the edge of a wood overlooking the water was a favourite place by which to dally. This is the Temple of Milton, whose bust adorns a niche inside. On the wall is an inscription from *Paradise Lost*:

Overhead upgrow
Insuperable height of loftiest shade
Cedar and fir and pine and branching palm
A sylvan scene and as the ranks ascend
Shade above shade, a woody theatre
Of stateliest view.

It is as if Milton had Mount Edgcumbe in mind when he wrote these lines.

Beyond, on the lower slopes of the park leading down to the sea, lie three formal flower gardens. The rambling English garden is predictable enough, with fine specimen trees and shrubs dotted about the lawns and traditional herbaceous borders. The French garden, in contrast, 'is a little square enclosure bounded by a high cut hedge of evergreen oak and bay and laid out in a parterre, with a basin and *jet d'eau* in the midst, issuing from rock-work intermixed with shells'. The parterre consists of impeccably clipped low box hedges arranged in a pattern and crammed with flowers - bright yellow and orange wallflowers in spring, red begonias in summer.

Nearby is a small rock garden full of surprises. Fragments of columns and capitals from Greece and Rome stand cheek by jowl with tiny tombstones in memory of animals beloved by the Edgcumbes. Should the visitor wish to rest, he can pause at Thomson's Seat, a pedimented alcove with Tuscan columns dedicated to the eighteenth-century poet James Thomson. Thence to the Italian garden: 'This plot of ground,' says the guide-book, 'is disposed in a regular manner with gravel walks, all meeting in the centre at a basin of water, in the midst of which is a beautiful marble fountain.' At one end of the garden two diagonal flights of steps lead to a white balustraded terrace decorated with classical ornaments. The graceful silhouettes of Apollo Belvedere, the Medici Venus, and Bacchus stand out against the dark green hedge of ilex and bay behind. An eighteenth-century orangery flanks the opposite end of this cool and elegant retreat.

Mount Edgcumbe illustrates the divergent trends of eighteenth-century garden design. It is part Garden of Artifice embellished with 'Gothick', 'Classick' and 'Rustick' buildings and planted with decorative flowering shrubs from far and wide and part romantic garden planted with native trees, and designed to appear untouched by human hand. These 'wild' places together with the craggy coastline that forms a grand but natural boundary to the gardens, made Mount Edgcumbe a rival to Stowe and Bleinheim as a tourist attraction.

Today Mount Edgcumbe's **Park** belongs to the Plymouth City and Cornwall County Councils and it is open all the year round. It is now the home of the National Collection of camellias and the recent creation of an American and New Zealand garden marks a new stage in the development of this historic landscape.

Mount Edgcumbe today. The Gothic folly overlooking Plymouth Sound.

Antony House 1711-21. The south front and forecourt. Engraving from *Natural History of Cornwall* (1758) by William Borlase.

ACROSS the water, to the north-west of Mount Edgcumbe, lies **Antony House**, the home of the Carew family since the late fifteenth century. In the 1540s, at about the same time as Sir Richard Edgcumbe was building his great house at Mount Edgcumbe, Thomas Carew married Sir Richard's daughter Elizabeth. Their son Richard married Juliana, daughter of Sir John Arundell of Trerice.

A portrait of Richard Carew, painted when he was thirty-two, hangs in the hall at Antony. Unlike many of his Elizabethan contemporaries, who chose to sit for their portraits in sumptuous apparel, Richard is dressed in black and wears a gold chain around his neck. His hair is close-cropped and his eyes, at once sensitive and alert, are those of an intelligent man. Characteristically, he holds a book in his hand.*

Carew was a loving father - he and Juliana had ten children - and nothing seems to have given him more pleasure than to watch them grow up. He paints a charming, albeit idealised, picture of life at Antony. One of his favourite pastimes was fishing. He describes how he built a salt-water pond on the shore of the Lynher to which he would retreat whenever possible. The pond was surrounded by a palisade to keep out scavenging otters, and had a flood-gate in the corner nearest the sea to let in the salt water.**

Although the remains of Richard Carew's 'fishful pond' can still be seen, the house he knew has vanished. Richard's great-great-grandson William Carew pulled down the old Antony and built a fine early Georgian mansion in its place. Building began in 1711 and was completed in 1721. Tantalisingly, the name of the architect of this supremely elegant house has never been discovered. For a long time Antony was attributed to James Gibbs, architect of several London churches and some fine country houses such as Ditchley in Oxfordshire, but no mention is made of Antony in the documentation of Gibbs's work, nor is there any record of his having worked in Cornwall. However, a design in Gibbs's *Book of Architecture*, published in 1728, closely resembles the plan and elevation of Antony, so it seems reasonable to suppose that a pupil or follower of Gibbs may have been the architect.

The design of Antony is immensely satisfying. It consists of a two-storey solid block whose proportions and size are perfect, neither too long nor too high, large yet not too large. This simple shape, which gives the house its gravity and serenity, is softened in a number of ways. Both the south and north fronts have a central pediment which projects very slightly, stressing three out of the nine bays of each façade. There are two rows of straight-headed windows on each façade and no external ornament at all. The punctuation is subtle. The space between the three centrally placed windows is narrower than that between the group of three on either side. The eye is thus made to focus on the centre, while the simplicity of the overall design allows us visually to absorb the whole. The six dormer windows in the hipped roof are not placed exactly above the bays below but slightly to one side, introducing small out-of-key lines into the otherwise vertical and horizontal grid.

If both façades follow the same architectural pattern, they are completely different in feeling. The south or entrance front forms one side of a square forecourt. At right angles to it on each side are two low wings of red brick. These wings are connected to the house by a brick wall with quaint corner pavilions. A wrought-iron entrance gate in the middle of the fourth side is aligned with the main entrance of the house, now camouflaged by a porte-cochère added after 1838. The contrast between the ornamental red brick and the soft, pale grey of the unadorned façade, built of Pentewan stone from Mevagissey, lessens the formality of the approach and introduces a note of gaiety. The friendly little courtyard welcomes and protects, while the north or garden front commands. Unfettered by buildings on either side, it stands majestically on a terrace that leads down to a magnificent stretch of lawn. If you turn back to look at the house, you look *up* at it, as if to pay homage.

In the last decade of the eighteenth century the fashionable landscape gardener Humphry Repton made one of his famous Red Books for Antony. Due to improved roads and modes of transport, Cornwall was no longer the backwater it had been. Cornish gentry were as up-to-date and receptive to new trends as their counterparts elsewhere. They could now be leaders of fashion instead of followers. The Earl of St Germans had consulted Repton in 1792-3 and commissioned him to lay out the grounds of Port Eliot, a few miles further up the Lynher river. Repton realised that there were other clients for him in this hitherto uncharted territory, and lost no time in persuading the Carews to consult him. He was immensely excited by the picturesque possibilities afforded by the riverside sites of both properties.

Repton's Red Books always contained one sketch showing the property in its current state and another showing what it would look like if his designs were implemented. The lodge at Antony Passage and the lodge at the main gate resemble his drawings, but many of his ideas for embellishing the terrace and approaches to the house were not taken up. His basic landscaping principles were, however, followed (whether then or later is not known), and the result is a tribute to him. The impressive expanse of grass which stretches down to the water's edge, broken by pleasingly positioned groups of trees, creates a grand yet natural vista of great beauty. Shelter from the elements is so essential in Cornwall that few houses are allowed the privilege of a magnificent prospect. The view from the terrace at Antony is one of the most memorable. To the west of the lawns sweeping down to the river Lynher are magnificent magnolias and an elegant hedge of clipped yews which form an arched entrance into an enclosed flower garden laid out with four beds set round a sundial in the centre. Beyond is a small knot garden.

In addition to the house and formal gardens round it, the visitor can also explore a further hundred acres of woodland garden owned by a charitable land

Antony. The flower garden.

Cotehele valley garden and dovecote.

Mount Edgcumbe House.

Prideaux Place. The Grenville Room.

Prideaux Place. The library.

Trerice. The east front.

Trerice. The drawing-room.

trust established by the Carew-Pole family who still live at Antony. Grassy paths meander through groves of camellias, rhododendrons, azaleas and magnolias and acers which flourish in a semi-wild setting. To the east of the woodland garden car park are a further fifty acres of older natural woodland with attractive walks along the banks of the river Lynher.

The interior of Antony, as harmonious as its exterior, has altered little since the house was built. Most of the rooms on the ground floor are panelled with Dutch oak, whose rich brown colour gives them warmth and intimacy. The main staircase, also of Dutch oak, has turned balusters and Corinthian columns for newel posts. These are lit at each turn by their original bubble lights, early eighteenth-century blown glass globes.

With the exception of one or two Elizabethan pieces in the hall, which probably came from old Antony, most of the furniture is contemporary and some of it has never left the house. The flavour of each room is unmistakably English - sober, restrained and sensible. The Carews were enthusiastic and discerning patrons of English portraitists and craftsmen. On the staircase hang portraits of the Carew, Pole and Coventry families (Lady Anne Coventry married Sir William Carew, the builder of the house) by Kneller, Beach, Northcote, Lely, and Hudson. Two full-length portraits of the 8th and 9th Earls of Westmorland by Reynolds hang in the saloon. But the most moving picture is that of Charles I by Edward Bower, thought to have been a pupil of Van Dyck and employed to sketch the King during the trial proceedings at Westminster Hall. Bower shows him dressed in black and clutching his silver-topped cane. He looks dignified and authoritative, yet his tightly pursed lips and inquiring eyes betray his apprehension.

A FEW miles upstream, on the west bank of the river Tiddy which flows into the Lynher just south of the village of St Germans, stands **Port Eliot**, the seat of the Earls of St Germans. The name is thought to come from St Germans of Auxerre who is known to have visited Britain in the fifth century, although there is no firm evidence that he was in Cornwall. At all events, after the Saxon subjugation of Cornwall, King Edward the Elder established a Cornish diocese here with St Germans as its cathedral. In 1170 the priory of Secular Canons was replaced by a strict Augustinian community, for whom the existing church, with its grand Romanesque portal of seven concentric rings set beneath a pointed gable, was built.

The earliest reference to the old priory as *Porte Ellyot* occurs in 1573, ten years after John Eliot, a merchant adventurer engaged in trade in Plymouth, bought the land and priory buildings from the Champernowne family for £500. John Champernowne had been quick to seize the main chance when, to quote Carew, 'the golden shower of the dissolved abbey lands rained well near into every gaper's mouth'. After the required bowing and scraping, Henry VIII leased

Antony House. The north front. Tragically, the cedar on the left crashed in the January 1990 hurricane.

Elizabethan almshouses (restored) in the main street of St Germans.

the house and demesnes of St Germans to Champernowne in 1540. His son, Henry, made over the property to John Eliot.

The quaint **almshouses** which flank the main street of St Germans were built in John Eliot's time. It was an age when merchants wanted to affirm their status and their reputations as public benefactors, as well as to erect a personal memorial by building almshouses. Eliot was evidently anxious to be remembered by posterity, for he stipulated in his will that the fine carved panelling he had installed in some of the rooms of *Porte Ellyot* was not to be removed.

John's nephew Richard inherited, but it was his successor, another John Eliot, who increased the family's wealth by marrying a rich yeoman's daughter with sizeable lands.*

Until the end of the eighteenth century, both church and house stood above marshes that bordered a tidal creek. However Edward Eliot, created 1st Lord Eliot in 1784, decided to reclaim an area of park from the mud flats and by the time he consulted Repton in 1792 the operation was well under way. He had already planted extensively on the ridge of high ground overlooking the river to the north and in the pleasure grounds on the promontory to the east. When discussing his plans for Port Eliot in his Red Book, Repton acknowledged Lord Eliot's skill and 'the tuition of that Judgement, Taste and persevering Energy which have not only clothed the naked hills with flourishing plantations, removed mountains of earth and vast beds of rock . . . but the waters of the neighbouring Ocean, converting into a cheerful Lawn that which was occasionally a bed of ooze . . .'

Today mature beeches and flowering shrubs adorn the slopes of the promontory, and the grand sweep of parkland culminating in the high point of the ridge known as the Craggs is as impressive as Repton would have wished. But sensibilities have changed. Whereas Repton's 'powers were subdued' on viewing the 'sublime horrors of the Craggs', we enjoy the prospect for its gentle natural beauty.

Repton's Cornish clients were stubborn individuals, for here, as at Antony, many of his recommendations were rejected. He wanted to link the house and church, in accordance with his principle of creating a harmonious whole, and proposed 'a cloister gateway' consisting of a billiard room above and a passage leading to the family pew below. Lord Eliot dismissed this idea and ten years later, in 1802, called in the London architect John Soane to remodel the house. Soane had already carried out alterations to Lord Eliot's London house in Downing Street, and Eliot was sufficiently pleased with the result to summon him to Cornwall, initially to advise on repairs to the church which had partially collapsed.

Lord Eliot died shortly afterwards in 1804 and it was left to his son, created Earl of St Germans in 1815, to supervise operations. Soane entirely remodelled the east front, which had originally consisted of the prior's hall and parlour. The house had already been modernised in the Georgian era. Soane retained the sash windows and mansard roof but gave Port Eliot a mediæval air, in keeping with its origins, by adding a battlemented parapet all the way round. At this time the east side of the house was the entrance front, the approach being from the quay and through the pleasure grounds. As time went on access by land became more convenient, and the 2nd Earl employed the architect Henry Harrison to make the present day west entrance-front in the 1820s.

A DESCRIPTION of **Trerithick**, a small manor house half way between the hamlets of Altarnun and Polyphant just west of Launceston, will give a more balanced view of East Hundred, where so many of the great Cornish families chose to live. It was built by a well-to-do farmer called John Hec in 1585, as the inscription above the entrance porch records. The ground plan follows the traditional mediæval pattern of hall, parlour, cross passage, and service room, but the rooms are lighter and more spacious than usual. Plain, flat-headed windows have replaced the round-headed type common in Tudor times, a few of which can still be seen in the outbuildings scattered round the house. The entrance porch, no longer a pointed Gothic arch but flatter and more rounded, has heavy roll-moulding running up the jambs and around the spandrels. The local stone carver has placed a single ball inside each spandrel. Granite lends itself to these bold, uncomplicated motifs; their honest simplicity gives this Cornish farmhouse its charm.

Houses like Trerithick, of limited value architecturally, are most revealing historically. They are the product of the Great Rebuild, that period in English history, *c.* 1580-1620, when a rise in population and an increase in wealth resulted in a building boom. When there was cash to spare, the middle classes chose to add on and improve, rather than to build new houses. Here the two-storeyed hall was abandoned in favour of a single-storey room with a bedchamber above; large fireplaces replaced the open hearth; more domestic rooms were added at the back of the house and larger windows, glazed rather than shuttered, were installed as time went on. Half veiled by the high stone hedge of an impossibly narrow lane, solid and unpretentious, Trerithick is an integral part of the Cornish heritage.

Port Eliot. 19th-century
engraving of the west front,
designed by
Henry Harrison c. 1829.

Trerithick, Altarnun.
The entrance porch bears
the date 1585.

3.
Lesnewth

and on the night
When Uther in Tintagil past away
Moaning and wailing for an heir, the two
Left the still King, and passing forth to breathe,
Then from the castle gateway by the chasm
Descending thro' the dismal night — a night
In which the bounds of heaven and earth were lost —
Beheld, so high upon the dreary deeps
It seem'd in heaven, a ship, the shape thereof
A dragon wing'd, and all from stem to stern
Bright with a shining people on the decks,
And gone as soon as seen. And then the two
Dropt to the cove, and watch'd the great sea fall,
Wave after wave, each mightier than the last,
Till last, a ninth one, gathering half the deep
And full of voices, slowly rose and plunged
Roaring, and all the wave was in a flame:
And down the wave and in the flame was borne
A naked babe, and rode to Merlin's feet,
Who stoopt and caught the babe, and cried 'The
King! Here is an heir for Uther!'

Alfred Lord Tennyson, *Idylls of the King*, 1859

THE savage, jagged cliffs and wild countryside round Tintagel have excited both the admiration and the awe of travellers over the centuries. John Norden, in his *Description of Cornwall* written in the first decade of the seventeenth century, finds the village of Tintagel 'a poore decayde place, furnished with a few decayde howses', and Botreaux (now Boscastle) where once stood a fine castle, 'a meane market towne and inhabited for the moste parte by poore men'. **Tintagel Castle**, once impregnable, is now 'rent and ragged by force of time and tempestes'. Indeed most buildings in Lesnewth, according to Norden, have fallen into decline and poverty with the demise of these two mighty seats.

More than two hundred years later, a nineteenth-century observer, Dr Maton, finds the surrounding countryside just as bleak and rugged but 'the whole forms such a dismal picture of desolation that we began to imagine ourselves removed by enchantment out of the region of civilisation'. If the dark, cavernous inlets and lashing waves depressed and terrified poor Norden, they thrilled the romantic mind which yearned to lose itself in the immensity of untamed nature.

Tintagel, with its ancient ruined castle half on a cliff, half on a rocky headland, is a supremely romantic site. The restless sea forever pounding against the castle walls reminds man of his helplessness in the face of the elements; the brutal grandeur of the scene raises it from the ordinary to the sublime. Fear was a favourite romantic emotion, and the very real danger of a shipwreck lured many a nineteenth-century tourist to Tintagel's treacherous shore. Today it is the myths surrounding Tintagel Castle as well as the dramatic setting which draw the crowds.

The actual history of Tintagel is as fascinating as the legends which have grown up around it. The headland provided good pasture land for the earliest settlers, who farmed there until about 350 AD. But when St Juliot, a Celtic missionary thought to have come from South Wales, arrived in the sixth century, this farming community had already gone. Excavations of the monastery he founded have revealed the remains of a sophisticated complex of buildings which included an infirmary and libraries. There is evidence that the settlement had running water and a primitive form of central heating. A Celtic granite tomb shrine which houses relics or possessions associated with St Juliot was uncovered in one corner of a Norman chapel built over the monastic site in the twelfth century. Coins, such as a silver penny of the reign of King Alfred the Great (871-99 AD), and fragments of 'red-gloss' pottery imported from Gaul or made in Britain, bear witness to a simple but flourishing monastic community whose life revolved round labour in the fields, services in the chapel, and the teaching of the peasants. Saxon domination brought peace and prosperity to an end, the monks left and the headland was once more uninhabited.

The Normans recognised the importance of the site. Building was begun by Reginald de Dunstanville, one of Henry I's illegitimate sons and Earl of Cornwall, in the 1140s. The chapel on the highest point of the headland, almost 100 metres above sea-level, and the walls of the great hall date from this time. Geoffrey of Monmouth, writing in the twelfth century, states: 'Tintagel Castle is situated upon a massive headland surrounded by the sea on every side, with but one drawbridge entrance to it, through a straight rock which three men shall be able to defend against the whole power of the kingdom'.

On Reginald's death in 1175, the castle was leased to local lords. No further building took place until 1236, when Richard, Earl of Cornwall and brother of Henry II, repossessed the castle and enlarged it. He built two wards on the mainland, the upper one containing the round keep, and constructed a massive curtain wall which embraced both island and mainland. The mainland wards provided accommodation for the earl's soldiers as well as stabling for the horses; the island quarters consisted of the great hall, eighty feet long, the private apartment of the earl, and the kitchens and buttery. By mediæval standards it offered an unbeatable defensive position and comfortable living quarters.

Like other Norman strongholds in Cornwall, Tintagel was in a sorry state when the Black Prince, as 1st Duke of Cornwall, claimed it in 1351. Part of the mainland site was used as a state prison in the late fourteenth century, but after that the buildings began to crumble. John Leland, who travelled all round Cornwall, reported in 1535, that 'shepe now fede within the dungeon grounde and rabbits abounde' but that the drawbridge was still there. Soon afterwards, part of the slate cliffs must have collapsed and sent the wooden drawbridge crashing into the sea. When Norden arrived on the scene in about 1600 he had to clamber down a perilously steep path to cross onto the island and up an equally precipitous cliff on the other side.

The leaste slipp of the foote sends the whole bodye into the devouringe sea and the worste of all is the higheste of all, neare the gate of the entrance into the Hall where the offensive stones so exposed hange over the head, as while a man respecting his footing he endangers the head and looking to save the head endangers the footing.

Even sheep, he comments morosely, who climb the cliffs like goats, sometimes miss their footing and hurl headlong into the sea.

Elizabeth I, anxious to strengthen coastal fortifications against the possibility of a Spanish invasion, ordered Sir Richard Grenville to survey Tintagel Castle, but although he reported that the ruins could be made fit for occupation the work was never carried out. Decay continued until the mid nineteenth century when an energetic vicar, the Revd R. B. Kinsman, took the parish of Tintagel in hand and cleared away the undergrowth which by then had covered the ruins.

Tintagel has been associated with King Arthur since the twelfth century, when Geoffrey of Monmouth, in his *History of the British Kings*, set King Arthur and his court, in the castle. In reality, King Arthur was probably a sixth-century Celtic chieftain who bravely rallied his countrymen to resist the Saxon invaders, but such was the popularity of both Monmouth's story and Sir Thomas Malory's *Le Morte D'Arthur* (which drew heavily on Monmouth), published in 1485, that most people came to think of Arthur as a mediæval king whose gallant knights embodied the ideals of chivalry and honour. He has remained a hero in English eyes, a symbol of goodness and strength. Tennyson revived the legends in verse in his best-selling *Idylls of the King* (1859), and kept Tintagel as the traditional birthplace of Arthur.*

The early Norman church of St Merteriana still stands on the bleak cliff, buffeted by the wind, and from the doorway you can look down at the castle on the headland and out to sea. To a rational mind it is merely a majestic view; for a lover of poetry, music and legend, the ruins of Tintagel Castle inspire tumultuous thoughts and dreams.

The ruins of Tintagel Castle (mid-13th century).

A romantic 19th-century view of Tintagel Castle.

THE main street of Tintagel, mostly a depressing mixture of late Victorian and Edwardian dourness and modern garishness, brings us back to reality with a bump. But in the same street the **Old Post Office**, a small but remarkably preserved mid fourteenth-century manor house reminds us of our Plantagenet past. Both walls and roof are built of local slate, now mellowed to an attractive grey-brown. The square chimney-stacks, the main one built in three tiers, are capped with four up-ended slates, apparently the local pattern of chimney-pot but now rarely seen. The roof bulges and dips because the heavy slates have made the supporting beams sag.

Inside a passage runs from the porch to the tiny garden at the back of the house. A door to the right leads into the parlour, possibly the original kitchen, with a narrow staircase leading to the bedchamber above. The occupants would have enjoyed gazing up at the wooden rafters bent into a comforting arc above their heads. An even narrower stair made of slate slabs set into the wall leads to a gallery overlooking the hall on the other side of the passage. This small area, lit by a tiny window and cut off from the hall by a wall of timber and plaster, was probably another bedchamber. To the left of the entrance passage is the hall, two storeys high and open to the roof timbers. The hearth has a huge grey-blue slate overmantel, an attractive contrast to the white-washed walls. A spiral staircase leads to a third bedroom, below which is the Post Room, complete with counter and receiver, just as it was in Victorian times.

In the early nineteenth century there was no post office in remote Tintagel. Letters were delivered on foot from Camelford, some six miles away.When Sir Rowland Hill introduced his Penny Postage in 1840, more and more people wrote letters more and more frequently – to the inconvenience of the overburdened postman trekking across the hills from Camelford. So in 1844 the GPO set up a Letter Receiving Office in Tintagel, and rented one room for the purpose from the owner of this old manor house. It served as the village post office for the next fifty years, until the then owner decided to sell the house. The Old Post Office, as it was then called, was put up for auction in 1895. An artist, Miss Catherine Johns, bought the house, as she was alarmed at the thought that it might be pulled down and replaced by a tawdry hotel. This was becoming the fate of many other cottages, for Tintagel was already a tourist Mecca for Victorian romantics acquainted with the poems of Tennyson, Arnold and Swinburne. Sales of pictures by a group of fellow artists were held to raise money for repairs. The National Trust purchased the Old Post Office in 1903 for £100 and has cared for it ever since.

HIGH on a nearby hill, above the coast road from Tintagel to Boscastle, stands the even older stone farmhouse of **Trewitten**, dating from the thirteenth century. It is a late version of a long house, having two storeys, 'two up and two down'. The larger ground-floor room provided living quarters for the family, with the later addition of a fireplace and stone newel stair in a rectangular turret to reach the room above, while the smaller downstairs room was originally a cattle byre.

FURTHER up the coast, a mediæval **Church House** survives in **Poundstock**, a picturesque village a mile or so from the sea. Built in the late fourteenth century, it is a two-storeyed rectangular building complete with stone buttresses (added early this century) and four-light casement windows made of oak. In order to raise money for the little church tucked away in the trees above the church house, the church wardens used to give revels in the upper room. Beer was brewed downstairs and sports were held in the graveyard behind, there being no gravestones at that time. Mummers' plays were part of the festivities and fairs were also held, the merchants setting up their stalls in the room downstairs and round the walls. In the sixteenth century the church house became the parish almshouse, and today the upper floor is still used for village meetings and to celebrate Harvest Festival. For some reason church houses are peculiar to this area of Cornwall only, and none save this one in Poundstock has survived.

TWO miles east of Poundstock lies **Penfound Manor**. The Revd Sabine Baring-Gould, vicar of Lew Trenchard just across the Devon border, wrote in *An Old English Home* (1898) 'in a dip in the land, at the source of a little stream, snuggling into the folds of the down, bedded in foliage, open to the sun, hummed about by bees, twinkled over by butterflies, lies this lovely old house', the home of the Penfound family from the early fourteenth to the mid-nineteenth century.

The earliest official record of the manor is in the Domesday Book, when it belonged to William the Conqueror's half-brother Robert, Count of Mortain. Called Penfou in Domesday (meaning head or source of the stream) it was known as Penfound by the sixteenth century. It is not known exactly when the de Penfounds took over the manor, but documents indicate that they were in residence in the reign of Edward III.*

As the Penfounds grew richer, so the house increased in size. In early Norman times it consisted merely of the great hall, two walls of which remain, more than six feet thick. The existing chimney and fireplace were probably added in the early thirteenth century. The scarlet and blue glass in the border of the Elizabethan window (to the left of the porch) came from Westminster Abbey after the second World War, when fragments of Abbey glass were made available for restoration work.

The first addition to the house was the Norman wing built at right angles to the south-west corner of the great hall. It consisted of a withdrawing-room for the ladies downstairs and solar above, reached originally by a stone spiral staircase. The women of the household could sit by the large mullioned window (which still retains its original glass) and enjoy the sun in this south-facing wing. The solar was the only bedroom until 1589, when the main staircase was built

The 14th-century Church House, Poundstock.

Penfound Manor, Poundstock. The entrance porch bears the inscription 'In the Yeare 1642' and the initials of Arthur and Sibella Penfound.

and a second bedroom added over the mediæval buttery, the first room to be built to the east of the screens passage. While the great families abandoned their fortified castles for magnificent mansions during this period of rising prosperity, country squires made their modest manors more comfortable, better heated, and better lit. Penfound was no exception.

No further building took place until 1635, when Arthur Penfound added a dairy and a new kitchen with bedrooms over each. He also laid a pebble path which runs from the porch, through the screens passage, to beyond the back door. He incorporated the date, 1638, in white pebbles at the entrance. Horses could now be taken straight through the house to be watered at the horse-trough over the well, instead of having to be led round the outside of the courtyard. The spandrels of the carved granite archway bear the initials of Arthur and his wife Sibella. The inscription 'In the Yeare 1642' is carved across the lintel. Arthur's son Thomas, a royalist like his father, planted a Judas tree in the courtyard on January 30th, 1649 to record his hatred of Charles I's executioners. The tree was struck by lightning in the 1930s and a sundial now stands in its place. Another Judas tree has been planted near the entrance gateway.

The Penfounds never knew great wealth — perhaps they were not grand enough to attract an heiress, nor sufficiently ambitious to seek distinction outside Cornwall — which accounts for the modesty of the successive alterations. Their fortunes went up and down, as happens to most families, and they suffered financially for their support of the Pretender in 1715. The last Penfound died in the Poundstock poor-house in 1847 'leaving issue in the state of poverty'. Fortunately, no subsequent owner enlarged the house, as so many Victorians were wont to do, and it remains an outstanding example of a mediæval manor house with sixteenth and seventeenth-century improvements. Looking through the wrought-iron gates into the quiet courtyard, now gay with geraniums and pink hydrangeas and down the path to the house itself, with its uneven slate roof and welcoming porch through which horses once passed, it is as if time has stood still at Penfound.

4.
West

And have they fixed the where and when
And shall Trelawny die
There's twenty thousand Cornish men
Will know the reason why.

R. S. Hawker

THREE rivers run the length of West Hundred, a small area sandwiched between East Hundred and Powder Hundred on the south coast. The river Fowey forms a natural boundary to the west, the river Seaton to the east. In between flow the river Looe and its tributaries. These three lushly-wooded river valleys cut through otherwise barren countryside, and great estates grew up in or near them.

Glynn stands high on a hill above the river Fowey, not far from Liskeard. Glynn is a Celtic word meaning valley, and the family who settled here soon after the Conquest took the same name. Centuries later, in 1805, Edmond John Glynn built a massive square late Georgian mansion on the site of the old one.

The heavy eaves and small windows (compared with those of Georgian houses elsewhere in England) of the south front show the architect's desire to protect this exposed side of the house, which looks right down the valley. On a rainy day the mist swirls up the hillside like some silent, stealthy spirit come to envelop the house in a damp grey shroud; when it is fine the silvery granite sparkles in the sunlight and you can see down the parkland to the wooded valley bottom and into the country far beyond. Such a sense of space round the house, a rarity in a county where shelter is the first consideration, adds to the grandeur of Glynn. The elegant windows of the entrance front with their crisply carved urns look very graceful from a distance.

Edmond John Glynn lived in this magnificent mansion for only a few years. According to Gilbert in his *Parochial History of Cornwall* (1838), his uncle had him proclaimed a lunatic — he apparently spoke to no one but communicated his thoughts by writing — and thereby inherited Glynn. But his ill-gotten gain was not enjoyed for long. On a chilly November day in 1819 a fearful fire broke out which swept through the main block. A brew-house at the back of the house escaped the furnace, but otherwise only the external walls survived. It was this huge stone shell which a dashing young cavalry officer bought in 1825.

Sir Hussey Vivian had returned victorious from Waterloo with numerous military decorations. He was determined that his new home should celebrate his achievement and honour his name. The portico of the entrance front and the giant columns of granite of the west front, otherwise built of cream-coloured

Glynn, near Cardinham.
The house was gutted by
fire in 1819 and remodelled
by Sir Hussey Vivian
soon afterwards.

Glynn. The drawing-room
window to the left of the
porticoed entrance.

Bodmin stone and part of the earlier house, are probably Sir Hussey's architectural contribution.

The west front looked on to a formal Italian garden with a fountain in the middle. A conservatory and octagonal pavilion were added to the façade during the Regency period. The drawing-room, little drawing-room and dining-room were all on this side of the house, their lofty ceilings decorated in the centre with beige and gold replicas in plaster of Sir Hussey's medals and orders. Although the Italian garden has long since vanished, the huge crimson rhododendrons and azaleas of the American garden, a large shrubbery on the slope above the formal flowerbeds, are still a sensational sight.

The Vivian family remained at Glynn until 1947, when the estate was sold. Neglected for over twenty years, the house was saved from demolition by its present owner who has restored it with great care. The glass roofs of the conservatory and pavilion, the latter a 'museum' where curios were displayed in the Vivians' day, were sensibly removed but the stonework preserved. Now a pink clematis trails over the remaining structure and plants replace copper pans on the stone shelves of the dairy behind.

A FEW miles from Lostwithiel and just south of Glynn lies another great estate. **Boconnoc** was the seat of the Carminows from very early times, but passed to the Courtenay family when a Carminow daughter married Sir Hugh Courtenay some time in the fifteenth century. Henry VII bestowed the title of Earl of Devon on Sir Hugh's son, Edward Courtenay — the title was forfeited when Thomas Courtenay, Earl of Devon, was beheaded for his Lancastrian sympathies after the battle of Tewkesbury in 1471. Edward's son married, as Henry VII had done, a daughter of Edward IV, so that his heir, created Marquis of Exeter, was a first cousin of Henry VIII and a potential claimant to the throne. Not surprisingly, he was arrested in 1538 and executed on a trumped-up charge of treason. All his estates became vested in the Crown, including Boconnoc, which was not long afterwards granted to the Russell family.

In 1579 the Russells sold Boconnoc to William Mohun whose descendants lived there for over a hundred years until in 1712 Sir William's great grandson, Charles, was killed in a duel.*

Five years later, Charles Mohun's widow sold Boconnoc to the late Governor of Madras, Thomas Pitt, who raised the purchase price by selling the fabulous Pitt Diamond which he had bought from a native in 1702. This was sold to the Regent of France, Philippe D'Orleans, for the princely sum of £125,000 and was eventually set in the hilt of Napoleon's sword. Pitt remodelled Boconnoc House, adding a new wing to the old structure. This east wing, with its elegant neo-classical dining-room, adorned with shell niches and pedimented doors, looked towards the little church of Boconnoc which stands on a bank just above the house.

Boconnoc. An early 19th-century engraving.

Boconnoc, near Lostwithiel. The east front.

Boconnoc. View from the south front, showing part of the six-mile-long
drive laid out by the first Lord Camelford.

Boconnoc. A picturesque waterfall in the woods.

Governor Pitt's great-grandson, the 1st Baron Camelford, added a further south wing overlooking the vast expanse of lawn and adjoining parkland. This wing contained an immense gallery on the upper floor where hung a magnificent collection of portraits. Lord Camelford was also a keen landscape gardener and an early enthusiast of the picturesque. He laid out a six mile drive through the oak and beech woods beyond the park, with sudden vistas of waterfalls, quaint bridges and grottos. The little river Lerryn, a tributary of the river Fowey fed by numerous streams, curls its way through the grounds so that the sound of running water is never far away. Today, the massive clumps of rhododendrons in the woods are an unforgettable sight in May.

High on a hill behind the house is an obelisk 123 feet tall, erected in 1771, in memory of Lord Camelford's uncle Sir Richard Lyttelton. It stands in the middle of an old military entrenchment that goes back to the Civil War.*

Walking through Boconnoc woods, home of the buzzard and the badger, and up to Boconnoc House high on its knoll, it is comforting to think that King Charles, whose fortunes were so soon to turn, enjoyed a month of safety here. Even nature was in sympathy with him. Legend has it that while King Charles was receiving the sacrament beneath the boughs of an old oak tree on which his standard was displayed, a shot was fired which narrowly missed him. The bullet struck the oak, which for ever afterwards grew in the most stunted fashion and sprouted mottled leaves. This oak was cut down by the uncle of the present owner, but another has been planted in its place.

In 1804, Lord Camelford's son Thomas was killed in a senseless duel in London at the age of twenty-nine. Boconnoc passed to Thomas's elder sister Anne Pitt. She had no children and it then went to her husband's nephew, George Matthew Fortescue, of Castle Hill in North Devon. Fortescues have lived at Boconnoc ever since, although no longer in the big house which is now empty.**

AS at Boconnoc, **Morval** house and church stand close together, tucked out of sight down a sleepy lane on the outskirts of Morval village, two miles north of Looe. In days gone by a boat would have brought a visitor up the River Looe as far as the lock about a mile from the house, which stands at the head of rich woodland further up the valley. A stream flows through the woods and widens into a small lake or inlet before joining the river, so that the grounds have great natural beauty. Trees on a hillside behind the house give shelter while on the other side grassy slopes stretch down to undulating parkland.

Morval originally belonged to the Glynn family, evidently relatives of the Glynns of Glynn since both families bore the same coat of arms. Feuds were common in Tudor times and Morval was the scene of a particularly vicious one, which led to the murder of John Glynn.†

Despite this tragedy the Glynns lived on at Morval until well into the sixteenth century, when Thomasine Glynn brought the manor in marriage to Richard Coode. In 1637 John Buller, younger son of the MP for Shillingham in Devon, married the last of the Coodes. He and his descendants occupied Morval for 250 years. His son John Francis increased the family's wealth and standing when he inherited Shillingham from his elder brother.

Retaining the shape of the original E-shaped block, Morval is a pleasing two-storied house with large four-light mullioned windows and simple hood mouldings. It was built largely in the seventeenth century, when the Bullers came to live there, but the white criss-cross roof, too, probably belongs to this later period. A low, buttressed wall bordered by flowerbeds encloses the terraced walk along the front of the house in a neat rectangle, the two slightly projecting wings providing additional shelter and privacy. To the right of the house stands the small, low church of St Wenna, half hidden behind the rhododendrons, where Glynns, Coodes and Bullers lie buried.

The last of the Bullers died childless in 1890, and Morval passed through the female line to the Tremayne family. It has been well maintained every since.

THE manor of **Trelawne**, just outside the village of Pelynt, to the west of Looe, was once the home of one of Cornwall's most illustrious families, the Trelawnys. The house, now a country club, has survived but the garden has been transformed into an amusement centre. Hard black tarmac has replaced the gravel paths and lawns that once surrounded Trelawne, its tranquil parkland now a noisy landscape of caravans, swimming-pools, children's slides and swings.

William Bonville lived at Trelawne in the fifteenth century, and the castellated towers of the semi-fortified Tudor dwelling can be seen on the eastern side. The rest of the house was rebuilt by Sir Jonathan Trelawny when he bought Trelawne in about 1600. A century later a chapel was erected on the south side, on the site of the old one, and a Georgian block with sash windows was added to the mediæval structure.*

Bishop Trelawny, the 3rd baronet, was by far the most colourful member of the family at Trelawne. He was a jovial character who fathered eleven children and had a reputation for swearing ('I do not swear as a priest but as a baronet and a country gentleman'). It is assumed that he inspired the poem with its rousing chorus 'And have they fixed the where and when and shall Trelawny die, there's twenty thousand Cornish men shall know the reason why', revived by Robert Stephen Hawker and now almost the national anthem of Cornwall.**

During the Trelawnys' long reign at Trelawne — they remained there until the beginning of this century — the West Looe river which threads its way through what was then Trelawny territory was an important waterway. The tide brought up plump salmon and gleaming sea-trout which were caught in a weir known as Shallow Pool and served at the baronets' dinner table.†

The Trelawne estate was broken up in the 1920s and the house became for a

Morval house and church, near Looe. 19th-century engraving.

Trelawne Manor, Pelynt. 19th-century engraving showing the Tudor castellated towers of the east side and the chapel built on the site of the old one c. 1700.

time a home for retired Church of England clergymen. Threatened with demolition in the 1950s, it is fortunate to have survived. The new owners of Trelawne were willing to meet the demands of a new age in which leisure, not industry, forms the basis of Cornwall's economy.

5.
Trigg

Aside from the town, [Bodmin], towards the north sea, extendeth a fruitful vein of land comprising certain parishes, which serveth better than any other place in Cornwall for winter feeding, and suitably enricheth farmers. Herethrough, sundry gentlemen have there planted their seats. . .

Richard Carew, *The Survey of Cornwall*, 1602

CAREW did not have a good word to say about Bodmin, deeming it to be the most 'contagiously seated' town in the county. The front rooms of the houses on the main street were dark and cold because a high hill blocked out the sun on the south side, while 'the back houses, of more necessary than cleanly service, as kitchens, stables, etc., are climbed up unto by steps, and their filth by every great shower washed down through their houses into the streets'. Nonetheless, Bodmin was a large and wealthy town in the Middle Ages, having been important as a religious community ever since St Petroc founded a monastery there in the sixth century.

Since very early times traders from Ireland, afraid of the treacherous seas round Land's End, would put into the port of Padstow and sail their boats up the Camel estuary to Wadebridge and beyond. They were then within striking distance of Bodmin. Cargoes of white fish, coarse Irish cloth for mantles, and prepared timber were taken the comparatively short distance overland to Lostwithiel, situated at the top of the Fowey estuary on the south coast. From there, the goods went by ship to Brittany. In return for Cornish tin, hides, herrings and pilchards, the Breton boats sailed into Fowey filled with salt, linen, woollen cloth, canvas and, most valuable of all imports, wine.

Situated midway between Padstow and Fowey, Bodmin benefited handsomely from its position along this trade route. Foreign merchants and traders attended its half-yearly fairs which, unlike ordinary markets, were festive occasions designed to draw people from far and wide. They offered a chance to see and buy foreign wares and to hear news from other parts of the county and indeed from England. Much later, Bodmin became a kind of central link in the road system. In the eighteenth century, stage coaches travelling east-west on the great mail road from Launceston to Truro and Falmouth or north-south from Camelford to Truro all stopped at Bodmin, which thus became an important crossroad.

Small wonder, then, that 'sundry gentlemen', to use Carew's words, chose to live near this prosperous and lively town where good conversation could be had and where friends from other parts of Cornwall frequently met. They could farm the fertile pockets of land towards the coast, involve themselves in county affairs, legal and administrative (the quarter sessions were held in Bodmin), and journey to London with comparative ease.

William Carnsew, who lived at **Bokelly** near St Kew in the latter half of the sixteenth century, was one such gentleman. A Tudor barn with hefty buttresses still exists, and a house too, although this was re-fronted towards the end of the seventeenth century. The view across the stubble fields to the skyline is the same now as it was in Carnsew's time. No other buildings have been erected, and a windy track still leads down to the house which is sheltered by a small copse.

According to Carew, William Carnsew was 'a gentleman of good quality, discretion and learning'. Surviving fragments of his diary for the year 1576-7 give a vivid picture of life at Bokelly. His preoccupations are those of an intelligent country squire, content to farm his land and visit his friends. Like any keen farmer, he notes weather conditions, takes an interest in sheep-shearing and the selling of wool, worries about his harvest of oats and wheat and the cutting of his meadows; like any Cornishman, he hears the wind and watches the sea. Three ships are cast onto the rocks, he reports, in a matter of a few days that stormy November.

In his spare time this jovial, gregarious man plays bowls, quoits, and saint with the locals, sets off on horseback along narrow lanes to stay with the Arundells at Lanherne or Trerice, or merely gallops across the fields to his neighbours the Roscarrocks at nearby St Endellion. Other friends lodge with him at Bokelly on their way to the assizes — Sir John Killigrew, for example, to whom Carnsew lends a fresh horse — or come to make merry on Twelfth Night. 'Many hawked with me,' he writes; 'George Grenville, Richard Carew, Richard Champernowne, their brethren.' They discussed current affairs as well as local matters over good food and wine. The Protestant and Catholic reaction to the Papal Bull that excommunicated Elizabeth I might have been one topic of lively conversation, for Carnsew's friends were from both camps.*

Old Carnsew was a devoted husband and father. His three sons were all at Oxford in the 1570s, the youngest, William, being made a Fellow of All Souls in 1579. They were a close-knit happy family. William wrote affectionate letters to his brother Richard at Bokelly from his chambers in London, hinting that he was finding it hard to make ends meet. His father visited him, bringing him money and, to his delight, books. His mother sent him new shirts, wondering as she sewed on the buttons, whether his landlady was feeding him adequately.

Young William was Member of Parliament for Camelford in 1597-8 and 1601. He relished the contact this gave him with Cornish folk and their affairs. In 1610 he married Ann Arundell of Trerice, a match that brought great pride and joy to his father who knew this respected family so well. But neither William nor his brothers Richard and Matthew produced children, and the Carnsew line came to

Bokelly, near St Kew. A Tudor
buttressed barn.

Bokelly, re-fronted towards the end of
the 17th century.

an end. Bokelly passed by sale to the Tregagle family in the mid-seventeenth century and ultimately became a Molesworth property. It is father Carnsew's diary, however, that brings Bokelly to life, and his spirit wanders there today.

A FEW miles to the north-west of Bokelly, between St Endellion and the coast, lies **Roscarrock**, which (according to Carew) 'in Cornish meaneth a flower, and a rock in English'. Little remains of the Tudor house that William Carnsew and Richard Carew used to visit, but among the outbuildings of the present late Georgian farmhouse is a range which testifies to the importance of Roscarrock. Above a secondary room on the ground floor is a large upper room with a four-light oriel window and an exceptionally handsome timbered roof. This must have been either a first-floor hall or a solar.

The history of Roscarrock is a sad yet noble one. The family were staunch Roman Catholics prepared to suffer for their faith. In 1577 Nicholas Roscarrock, a barrister and antiquary, was accused at Launceston assizes of failure to attend Protestant services; three years later he was imprisoned in the Tower and was not released until 1586. He joined Francis Tregian, another brave Cornish recusant, in the Fleet prison and whiled away the time by compiling an account of the British saints, translating the lives of a number of Cornish saints from the Cornish with which he was conversant.

Known adherence to Rome meant not only imprisonment but the risk of losing one's lands and possessions. Moreover, virtually no Catholic family, with the exception of the wealthy Arundells of Lanherne, could afford to pay the fine exacted by the government in the 1580s for non-attendance at church. The Roscarrocks lost everything, and their impoverished estate passed into the hands of the Crown. Nicholas never saw Cornwall again, and spent the last years of his life at Naworth with Lord William Howard. Distressed as they were to see him endure such hardships, his Protestant friends such as Richard Carew, who praised him most warmly in his *Survey* for 'his industrious delight in matters of history and antiquity', secretly admired his courage and the strength of his conviction.

A MILE to the north of Bokelly, just outside the hamlet of Trelill, stands **Pengenna**, a fine seventeenth-century farmhouse. It is said to have been built by the Revd Thomas Pocock, whose initials are carved over the entrance. Like so many other well-to-do farmers, the Pococks found the mediæval house dark, uncomfortable and constricting, and decided to build a new, spacious house against the old Tudor block. Built of the local rubblestone, it towers above the earlier house and looks exceedingly handsome with its mullioned windows and hoodmoulds.

The charm of Pengenna lies in the fact that it is built at right angles to the steeply-sloping land at one side. You approach it from behind. The rear elevation, with its tiny attic windows above the first floor and its stalwart buttress, seems

Pengenna, Trelill. The 17th-century entrance front built to the right of the old Tudor block.

Pengenna. The old Tudor block.

on the defensive and definitely forbidding. But as you walk past the Tudor block and turn into the courtyard, the smiling face of the front of the house bids you welcome, its Delabole slate roof glistening in the sun. Fine old outbuildings are clustered round the farmyard, from which you can look south down the wooded valley to Tremeer.

TREMEER GARDEN, just outside St Tudy, is a twentieth-century creation of outstanding beauty and of interest to any horticulturist. Eric Harrison, soldier and veteran of the First World War, bought Tremeer in a semi-derelict condition in 1939. More interested in hunting than in gardening — he was master of the North Cornwall hounds — it was not until after the war, when he retired from the army, that he devoted any attention to the garden. In 1946 Tremeer boasted only one magnolia, a few rhododendrons choked by nettles and brambles, and the remains of a herbaceous border. Some mature, deciduous trees gave shelter but that was about all. With the eye of an aesthete, Harrison realised the potential of the seven acres of ground he had acquired and set about transforming it.

The success of the overall design is immediately apparent. Nothing seems contrived, and yet wherever one strolls — down the gently sloping lawns towards the two ponds and mill-leat or across the grass to left or right — pleasing vistas and wonderful colour greet the eye. Evergreen oaks, *Cupressocyparis leylandii thuya* and *Griselinia littoralis*, as well as conifers and sweet bay, break up the broad swathe of lawn in a natural way, giving a sense of intimacy and variety. The trees are so placed that a number of different routes to the bottom of the garden are introduced. Walk straight down the middle of the lawn to an old oak tree — the ground beneath it a mass of wild cyclamen in September — or wander in a horizontal or diagonal direction across the grass into small clearings created by the trees. Whichever way you go, the bottom of the garden is a treasure-trove. After the subtle greens, pale and dark, a gawdy array of reds and pinks startles the visitor. Rhododendrons were Harrison's great love and he planted them in profusion. He learned how to grow them from seed or from cuttings and experimented with hybridisation quite early on. In fact he was so successful that the Royal Horticultural Society awarded him many prizes over the years. In 1961 Harrison married Roza Stevenson, the owner of Tower Court, Ascot, famous for its rhododendrons. Two hundred or so unwanted shrubs were shifted to Tremeer, where they now flourish magnificently. Nearly all are ticketed so that gardening enthusiasts can learn as they marvel at the achievement of one man and his gardener.

Harrison despaired of success because honey fungus, particularly virulent in the soft, moist Cornish air, attacked and killed many of the rhododendrons he planted. He turned to camellias as an alternative, planting them at random along the grassy paths that lead to the pond. In early spring this nonchalantly-planned

Tremeer Garden, St Tudy.
View from the terrace.

Tremeer Garden.

shrubbery is a breath-taking sight. The rhododendrons and camellias almost overhang the pond where ducks waddle and quack. It is shadier, more enclosed here; shafts of light through the trees dapple the water on a sunny day, and crimson petals make bright dots of colour on the surface as they float slowly by. Candelabra primulas, irises and moisture-loving perennials grow on the banks of the pond. Swans and deer made of lead are silent companions at the water's edge, guardians of the beauty around them.

As in most Cornish gardens devoted to camellias and rhododendrons, late summer colour is a problem. At Tremeer the solution is a wide border flanking the gravel path along one side of the house. This is filled with hydrangeas, eucryphias, enkianthus and embothrium, hypericums and heathers, which flower well into the autumn.

In the early fifteenth century the manor of Tremeer belonged to John Treffry. By 1570 it had passed to Edward Lower whose mother was a Treffry, and the Lower family was to remain here for more than a hundred years. Doctor Lower, Charles II's physician, was born at Tremeer and was rumoured to have carried out experimental blood transfusions on rats and dogs on the premises. Tremeer House was rebuilt in 1798 and altered extensively in about 1900 when an extra storey was added, which rather throws it out of proportion. The semi-circular bay windows of the garden front provide glorious views not only of the garden but of the rolling fields beyond. In the eighteenth and nineteenth centuries the house changed hands several times, but did not benefit in any way until Harrison arrived in 1939. Due to his imagination and expertise, and the present owners' hard work, Tremeer Gardens are superbly kept and lovely to behold.

PENCARROW, the grandest house in Trigg Hundred, lies just north of Bodmin at the head of a thickly wooded valley through which the river Camel flows. Pencarrow belonged long ago to the ancient families of Stapleton and Sergiaux and is thought to have passed from them to a family who took their name from it, the de Pencarrows. In 1497 a Pencarrow joined other Cornishmen in an ill-fated uprising against an unfair levy on tin. Branded as a traitor, he conveyed the estate to a neighbouring nobleman, Lord Marney of Colquite (near St Mabyn — the ruin of a late fifteenth-century house still exists below the present one), hoping that his influence might save his life. Pencarrow then passed to Lord Marney's heirs, an Exeter family named Walker, who sold it to John Molesworth during the reign of Queen Elizabeth. The Molesworth-St Aubyn family who own Pencarrow today are his descendants.*

The present house, an imposing, square Palladian-style mansion built in the 1760s by a young Yorkshire architect called Robert Allanson, stands at the end of a mile-long drive which is one of the loveliest in Cornwall. The visitor proceeds first past an Iron Age fortified encampment whose inner ditch is a perfect oval, and then into a wood of tall, stately beeches and old oaks, the

Tremeer, rebuilt in 1798 with an upper storey added c. 1900.

Pencarrow, near Bodmin. The entrance front c. 1760.

von Commercial

otos.

sunlight glinting through their branches, and making flickering shadows on the ground. Banks of deep cobalt-blue hydrangeas line the last part of the drive, which finally curves sharply round to the east front of the house.

After the natural woodland setting of the drive, the elegantly laid-out garden round two sides of the house comes as a surprise. A garden in Cornwall which even hints at formality is something of a rarity since so many are wild, romantic gardens carefully cultivated to appear as if they had never been touched by human hand.

Humphry Repton would have approved of Pencarrow's terraced flowerbeds round the house, its huge circular lawn, fountain and neat gravel paths. A garden, he said 'is a piece of ground fenced off from cattle and appropriated to the use and pleasure of man: it is or ought to be, cultivated and enriched by art, with such products as are not natural to this country'. At Pencarrow a straight gravel path leads from the central fountain and up two sets of steps to the parkland fence, beyond which cattle graze. The manicured lawn is surrounded, on a higher level, by mature shrubs set in a rock garden, the granite boulders heaved from Bodmin Moor being the only ornaments among the rhododendrons and camellias.

Trees have been carefully placed so as not to interrupt the vistas to the house, and blend naturally with the park scenery and woodland beyond. Here, outstanding specimens of the oriental spruce (*Picea orientalis*) and *Picea polita* (Japanese Tiger-tale spruce), conifers from America and monkey puzzles from Chile tower above both lake and drive. Planting on this grand scale began in the 1840s when the famous Veitch nursery near Exeter was obtaining seed directly from plant collectors such as David Douglas who brought back *Pseudotsuga menziesii* or Douglas fir, *Picea sitchensis*, the Sitka spruce and *Pinus ponderosa* and *Pinus radiata* from the west coast of America, and William Lobb who travelled in Brazil, Chile and California, returning with live plants of the Redwood Tree *Sequoia sempervirens*. These and countless other new introductions proved irresistible to Sir William Molesworth Bt., M.P. who, during Parliamentary recesses between 1831-55, supervised the planting of the drive and woodland as well as the laying-out of the sunken Italian garden in front of the house and the rockery. Fortunately, subsequent generations have continued to plant, introducing not only new specimen conifers from all over the world but also hundreds of different rhododendrons, camellias and other shrubs.

The interior of Pencarrow reflects the tastes of its owners over the past two hundred years. Friendly and knowledgeable guides who know the house and its history intimately, bring the rooms to life. The entrance hall was turned into a pine-panelled library by the 8th baronet in the first half of the nineteenth century. A display of porcelain, European and Chinese, deserves a close look, and in the same cabinet are a set of beautiful Georgian wine glasses with air-twist decoration in the stem, as well as an unusual collection of glass ink pens blown

Pencarrow. The drive.
Pencarrow. The drawing-room.

Lanhydrock house and gatehouse.

Lanhydrock. The higher garden.

Heligan. Flora's Green.

Heligan. The kitchen garden.

Trewithen. The north front.

Trewithen. Rhododendron 'Pink Pebble' in the great glade.

for the 1851 Great Exhibition.

The Molesworths were travellers who appreciated French and Italian modes of decoration. A canapé by Georges Jacob, with its original tapestry of roses, stands between the windows in the drawing-room, and the furniture is gilded in the French manner. The chairs and curtains are covered in deep musky pink flowered silk damask which was taken from a Spanish galleon captured off the Philippines. It was on its way to the Argentine with a cargo of Chinese silks. The admiral responsible for the operation was a relative of the 6th baronet who brought the silk back as a present. The dark *gros bleu* Sèvres plates and candelabra set on the white marble Adam chimney-piece show how effective a mixture of styles can be.

The rococo plasterwork of the music room ceiling is wonderfully light and airy. Its four corners depict the four seasons — daffodils for spring, corn for summer, grapes for autumn and fire for winter. The shell, bird and floral motifs of the overall design are so graceful that one suspects a French or Italian craftsman was at work.

A liking for the oriental is also evident, in fine examples of Chinese porcelain of the Kang Hsi period, and there is a rare Chinese cabinet in the drawing-room. Its interior is designed to look like a stage with tiny actors on it. The walls of an ante-room off the dining-room are covered in nineteenth-century hand-painted Chinese linen with a beautiful bird design in soft blues. A large bowl on a table depicts, on the inside, Pencarrow through Chinese eyes. Drawings of Pencarrow were sent over to China for the artists to copy, but they turned the house into a Palladian pagoda and the horses and hounds in front have decidedly slanted eyes!

Family portraits include an important series painted by Sir Joshua Reynolds in the dining-room, a full-length portrait of Sir Arscott Ourry Molesworth by Sir Henry Raeburn in the inner hall and a conversation piece by Arthur Devis painted in 1754 of the four Misses St Aubyn. On the upper staircase wall hangs a moving portrait of Charles I by Edward Bower who is said to have made sketches of the King at his trial before painting four variants of the monarch. It is interesting to compare this version with the one already mentioned at Antony.

Upstairs, Pencarrow has a more informal air. Regency and Victorian furniture appears in the bedrooms, which all look lived-in; wide-eyed, prettily dressed Victorian dolls are propped up on the pillows. The Molesworths seem to have held the view that 'one should hang on to everything', with the happy result that a dolls' house, perambulators, toys and dolls survive as souvenirs of childhood a century ago.

A MODEST, two-storeyed rectangular manor house called **Kirland** stands on a hill surrounded by tall, spindly trees full of cawing rooks on the outskirts of Bodmin. It is remembered fondly by Emma Gifford, Thomas Hardy's first wife, whose home it was in the 1860s. 'This little old manor-house has some good points about it,' she writes in her *Recollections*, which Hardy found after her death.*

Its stuccoed walls are painted a warm beige, and from the porch one looks down the sloping lawn to the stream and fields below and beyond. It has changed little in a hundred years.

Kirland, Bodmin. The home of Thomas Hardy's first wife, Emma Gifford.

6.

Pydar

Pydar in Cornish is Four in English, and this is the fourth hundred of Cornwall if you begin your reckoning from the western part, at Penwith.

Richard Carew, *The Survey of Cornwall*, 1602

ALTHOUGH Norden dismissed Pydar as a barren region of heath and turf that 'wanteth woode', it boasts some fine houses with interesting histories. Pydar is rich in Celtic memories because of its association with St Petroc, who founded a monastery on the southern banks of the river Camel in the sixth century — the site of Padstow today. Fierce Danish raiders ravaged Padstow in 981 and St Petroc's relics were moved to Bodmin, a safer inland site. The earliest record of Bodmin Priory dates from the mid eleventh century, and for the next five centuries, until the dissolution of the monasteries in 1536, it controlled vast estates in north Cornwall, including property in the Padstow area.

Rialton, which at first glance looks nothing more than a commonplace Cornish stone cottage, slightly larger than most, stands just off a narrow road outside St Columb Minor. The front of Rialton faces away from the road, but as soon as the visitor enters the little courtyard, it becomes clear that this is no ordinary dwelling but the main wing of a late fifteenth-century monastic manor, comprising a hall and kitchen with a solar above. The manor of Rialton is mentioned in Domesday when it had seven hides of land. The canons kept two hides and the villeins had the remaining five. There were also 60 acres of wood and 300 of pasture. In the early sixteenth century the priors of Bodmin decided to turn Rialton into a pleasant country residence. Prior Vyvyan, the last but one prior before the dissolution, added the wide porch with the study above. In two of the study's three six-light mullioned windows are fragments of glass with the initials TV — Thomas Vyvyan — and three fishes, the arms of the priory. Next to the study is the prior's oratory or bedchamber, which would once have had a fine view over the estate's meadows and orchards.

Prior Vyvyan died in 1533 and was succeeded by Thomas Mundy.⁎

Five generations of Mundys lived at Rialton until Parliamentarians seized the property during the Commonwealth. At the Restoration the Godolphins were granted the lease but never lived there, although the 1st Earl Godolphin took Viscount Rialton as a second title. Rialton became a farm and, in about 1870, when the Duchy built a new farmhouse further up the valley called Rialton Barton, became known as Rialton Mill. The east or service wing at right angles to the remaining one was then pulled down.

NICHOLAS PRIDEAUX was Prior Vyvyan's man of affairs and this association served him well. Acting upon the dying prior's wishes, he ensured that Secretary Cromwell appointed Mundy as Vyvyan's successor. Nicholas was duly rewarded by Mundy with the lease of the great tithes of the four parishes of Egloshayle, St Minver, St Cubert and Padstow. Tithes, mainly from churches whose rectories were appropriated to them were the other chief source of monastic income, but these, like the revenues from ecclesiastical estates, fell into the hands of the laity in the form of long leases which the Crown found impossible to repossess after the dissolution. Near the tithe-barn of the monks at Padstow, 'a new and stately house' according to Carew, was built by Nicholas Prideaux's great-nephew in 1592. It was called Place. 'Place' means palace, and other houses in Cornwall that were built on monastic property, such as Place at Fowey, bear the same name.

Prideaux Place, as the house is now called, is surrounded on three sides by belts of trees planted in the eighteenth century. The fourth side, or entrance front, looks across the deer park to the high ground on the other side of the Camel estuary. This long east front, with its three projecting bays, forms the characteristic Elizabethan E shape. Edmund Prideaux, son of the Dean of Norwich, who inherited Place in 1728, probably altered the façade slightly. A drawing of his shows that the projecting bays originally had pointed gables. It seems likely that it was he who removed these and extended the castellations in the horizontal line we see today.

The south front has been subject to many more changes, since the principal rooms, always the first to be altered to follow new fashions, are on this side. Another drawing of the 1730s by Edmund Prideaux, made before any alterations took place, shows that this side of the house was a simple two-storeyed rectangular block with five irregularly placed bays. This lack of symmetry no doubt offended the Georgian Edmund, who left another drawing with a scale at the bottom, presumably as his scheme for alteration. He retains the shape, but inserts two more bays — his windows are no longer two-light mullions but elegant sash windows — and continues the two string courses right the way along the façade to create a more classical effect. In 1810 the Revd Charles Prideaux-Brune added the square library tower at the left end of the façade and the round central tower or large bow of the drawing-room and principal bedroom above. The deliberate irregularity and decorativeness of the 'Gothick' windows and bobbly pinnacles create an informal, picturesque effect similar to that which Nash achieved in Luscombe in Devon ten years earlier. Since the removal of the top layer of the bow and all the pinnacles twenty years ago (they were no longer safe) the south front looks more uniform than intended. The Regency Gothic plasterwork of the drawing-room, library and hall ceilings remains. The late seventeenth-century panelling and carvings in the Grenville Room came from the the dining-room at Stowe after it was demolished. Recently decorated and regilded, it is a very handsome room.

Edmund Prideaux's drawing of the south front of Prideaux Place before any alterations took place *c*. 1730.

Prideaux Place. A second, scaled drawing by Edmund Prideaux *c*. 1730, showing his preferred scheme for alteration.

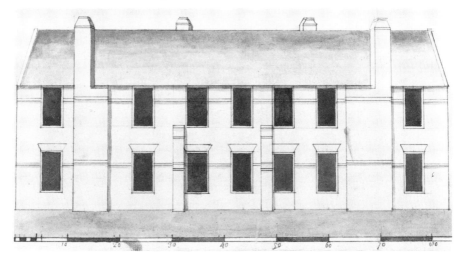

Prideaux Place. 19th century engraving showing the final scheme for the south front, carried out by the Rev. Charles Prideaux-Brune *c*. 1810.

Despite such alterations to the original interior, the Elizabethan lay-out can still be discerned. The entrance porch on the east front led into a screens passage with a single-storey great hall to the south. This was redecorated in the eighteenth century, presumably by Edmund, and the original screen removed. The existing screen, with its superbly inlaid frieze and panels of fantastic animals and floral designs (thought to be Spanish work of the late sixteenth or early seventeenth century), was probably fitted when the hall was turned into a dining-room in the nineteenth century. The great chamber, above the great hall, was split into two bedrooms in the eighteenth century. The original barrel-vaulted plaster ceiling, until recently concealed beneath a lower one, is well preserved. The delicately modelled panels depict the biblical story of Susannah and the Elders and are linked together by intricate strapwork and smaller panels framing birds and animals. The gallery at Lanhydrock, to be discussed later in this chapter, has a plasterwork ceiling of the same quality and style and clearly shows the same team of plasterers at work.

Edmund Prideaux was not only an amateur architect and interior decorator but also a keen landscape gardener. Following contemporary custom, he erected a number of small monuments in the grounds, including an Ionic temple, an obelisk and a grotto. He also built a small stone arbour to house a collection of Roman funerary urns acquired during his Grand Tour of Italy. His son Humphrey removed the obelisk, wishing to landscape the grounds in the natural manner favoured by 'Capability' Brown. He also added the castellated gateway and low battlemented wall that form such a romantic entrance today.

With help from the Cornwall Gardens Trust (a charity formed in 1988 to document and preserve historic Cornish gardens), the Prideaux-Brunes have recently restored the formal Victorian Italian garden and ornamental pond.

The stables, with their pretty Gothic windows and doors, were built by the Revd Charles as part of the alterations of 1810 and have survived intact. At the top of the stableyard is the dairy. This delightful building, in the course of restoration, has a square antechamber and an octagonal creamery with corbels in the shape of cows' heads supporting the ribbed ceiling. Here milk was poured into slate-edged settling dishes and left for a day to 'settle'. When the cream had risen to the surface and been taken off, the plug would be pulled out so that the thin, skimmed milk could run into a basin below. The dairy maid would then put the cream into a churn to make butter.

A THIRD house in Pydar with monastic origins is **St Benet's**, which can be seen from the road just outside Lanivet a few miles south west of Bodmin. An early fifteenth-century Benedictine foundation, originally a lazar house or hospital, it passed to the Courtenay family at the time of the Dissolution. Today, its fifteenth-century windows are incorporated into the mid-nineteenth-century façade. The two niches and small oriel window with their ogee heads also come

Prideaux Place. Edmund Prideaux's drawing of the east front and garden in the late 1730s.

St Benet's, Lanivet. The windows of the 15th-century Benedictine foundation are incorporated into the 19th-century façade, behind which stands the ruin of the old church tower.

from the original building. The tower of the original church can be seen at the back of the house.

Thomas Hardy's first wife, Emma Gifford, has left us a picture of St Benet's in her *Recollections*.⁘

The house deteriorated rapidly after Emma's time, but was restored by enterprising owners in the 1960s. It now looks beautifully kept, with an attractive garden in front. The old tower behind has rightly been kept a ruin, although the top storey has been altered, to remind us of its history.

THE beautiful Vale of Lanherne, the only richly wooded valley in Pydar, runs down to the sea at Mawgan Porth, half-way between Padstow and Newquay. It once belonged to the richest and most powerful family in Cornwall, the recusant Catholic Arundells of **Lanherne**. Just above the church in the village of St Mawgan, you can see the high walls that surrounded their home.⁘

Lanherne fell into decay in the early eighteenth century when the heiress of Lanherne married the 7th Lord Arundell of Wardour and left Cornwall. However in 1794 Henry, 8th Lord Arundell, who was responsible for the building of Wardour Castle as we know it today, generously assigned Lanherne to a group of English nuns who, upon the French invasion of Belgium, had been forced to leave Antwerp. The sisterhood has flourished here ever since, for Lanherne remains a convent to this day.

One can only glimpse the top of the late seventeenth and eighteenth-century parts at the back of the house from the other side of the high walls, but the Elizabethan entrance front can be approached from the little road that runs up the hill beside the church. Built long and low with its back to the hillside, it commanded extensive views over the valley below. Today this unassuming house which, but for the Arundell arms above the porch and on the gutter heads, gives no hint of its past magnificence, is camouflaged by surrounding orchards and trees. In the small garden by the main entrance stands a very fine early Christian cross. It is the fitting attribute of a house whose inmates so steadfastly followed the dictates of their faith and suffered for it. The nuns cherish its presence.

TRERICE, an important and well-preserved Elizabethan manor house about three miles south-east of Newquay, was for four hundred years the home of another family of Arundells. Closely related in the Middle Ages to the Arundells of Lanherne, the Trerice Arundells share the same coat of arms. Both bear six swallows and it is from the French *hirondelle* that the name derives.

Ralph Arundell married the heiress of Trerice in the fourteenth century and his descendant John, who died defending St Michael's Mount in 1471, was knighted for his services to the King. The family quickly became one of the most prominent in Cornwall. The 4th Sir John was the builder of Trerice. He married Katherine Coswarth, who brought with her substantial property in the adjoining

17th and 18th-century
additions at the rear of
Lanherne.

Lanherne. The entrance
porch with rainwater heads
bearing the Arundell coat
of arms.

parish. The actual manor house of Coswarth, however, was entailed on her great-uncle who had set about rebuilding it. Spurred on by his example, or anxious to outdo him, she and Sir John built the present Trerice at about the same time. Work was completed in 1573, a year before Sir John was appointed Sheriff of Cornwall. Richard Carew married their eldest daughter Juliana and often stayed at Trerice. He speaks so warmly of his father-in-law in his *Survey of Cornwall* that each visit must have been a pleasure. He describes the new buildings as 'costly and commodious', as they certainly were.

A small entrance court, at one time laid out with a formal lawn on either side of a central pathway and herbaceous borders along the walls, forms the approach to the house. Like the east front of Prideaux Place, the east façade of Trerice is E-shaped with three projecting bays, but a quite different visual effect has been achieved. It is built of a local limestone that has turned grey with time but is in fact of a yellowish hue. The curved gables are Flemish-inspired and similar to those at Montacute House in Somerset. All the windows of the façade are mullioned and transomed, the magnificent twenty-four light window of the hall occupying the whole of the space between the south gable and the porch.

Following the traditional mediæval English plan, a screens passage runs from front to back of the house, with the kitchen and service quarters on one side and the principal rooms on the other. The two-storeyed hall has a plaster ceiling decorated with oak leaves and scroll work. Strapwork divides the flat surface into an intricate pattern and curves downwards at intervals to form attractive globular pendants which catch the light streaming in from the enormous east window. The initials on the ceiling, JA, KA, and MA, are those of Sir John and Lady Arundell and his sister Margaret. Above the screens passage is a small minstrel's gallery off a corridor that runs across the centre of the house. A row of small arched openings set at cornice level enabled the musicians to look down into the hall below. There probably would have been a carved screen below the gallery originally, as at Prideaux Place, as well as wainscoting. This was removed some time ago and the walls are now plain white to match the ceiling.

The large drawing-room upstairs has always been the main sitting-room at Trerice. It was the solar of the Tudor house, but Sir John made it grander by using the attic space above to make room for the plastered barrel-vaulted ceiling we see today. It is covered with ornamental strapwork and above the frieze at one end of the room are the arms of Henry Fitz Alan, 24th Earl of Arundel and Knight of the Garter, who married Sir John's daughter Mary. The Trerice Arundells were pleased with this marriage and wanted it recorded for posterity. The huge plaster overmantel with more arms quartering other Arundell marriages is also contemporary and dated 1573. Almost identical plasterwork exists at Collacombe Barton near Tavistock in Devon.*

During the eighteenth century Trerice was let to tenants, but when Sir Thomas Dyke-Acland came into the property in 1802 he used it as his base whenever he was in Cornwall. The Aclands sold the estate in 1915 and it was acquired by the Cornwall County Council immediately after the First World War. The 500-acre manor farm was divided into lots which were sold off separately, leaving the house with twenty acres. This was finally bought by the National Trust in 1953 and has been maintained superbly ever since.

The formal Elizabethan gardens round the house have long since disappeared and the original designs are lost. Instead, the Trust has planted fruit trees on the south side, arranged in the quincunx pattern in favour during the seventeenth century, whereby each tree is aligned with the others from wherever it is viewed, and the herbaceous borders are memorable.

LANHYDROCK, another National Trust property, stands in its own magnificent park on the far western slope of the valley of the river Fowey as it turns southwards towards Lostwithiel and the sea. One of the largest houses in Cornwall, it was built in the 1630s by Sir Richard Robartes, a wealthy tin and wool merchant from Truro. Originally a monastic estate belonging to the Augustinian priory of St Petroc, it was obtained by the Glynn family at the time of the Dissolution. A Glynn daughter brought it in marriage to a James Lyttleton and his sister brought it to her husband Thomas Trenance. Their son, Lyttleton Trenance, sold Lanhydrock to the Robartes family in 1620. All these owners lived in a modest monastic barton which probably stood to the north-west of the little churchyard of St Hydroc church immediately behind the present house. But the Robartes made a fortune in the tin trade and Sir Richard Robartes, who paid James I's favourite, the Duke of Buckingham £10,000 in return for having him made a peer, set about building a grand new house. He did not live to see it finished and his son John, the 2nd Lord Robartes, completed the task.*

The architecture of Lanhydrock, essentially Tudor in appearance with its crenellated parapet, mullioned and transomed windows and pinnacles, shows what scant attention the 2nd Lord Robartes paid to new trends. After all, as leader of the Cornish Parliamentarians in the House of Lords and therefore often in London, he must have seen Inigo Jones's Banqueting House (1619-22) a few hundred yards away in Whitehall, but like most of his contemporaries failed to appreciate its grace and originality. Robartes preferred a house in an English rather than Italian mould. Built of the local pale grey granite, which does not lend itself to elaborate detailing, the exterior of Lanhydrock has only the simplest embellishments. The hood-moulds of its fine mullioned and transomed windows are joined right the way round the façade by a continuous string course whose horizontality is reinforced by the line of the parapet above. It is interesting to note that the north façade of Godolphin House in Kerrier shares these two features and is thought to be of mid-seventeenth century date.

The mansion originally consisted of four wings built round a quadrangle, the east wing enjoying views of the gatehouse and the great avenue of sycamores beyond. This whole wing was pulled down towards the end of the eighteenth century, leaving the three sides of the square we see today. At the same time the walls which flanked the gatehouse and enclosed a forecourt were removed. The gatehouse, with its ball-topped obelisks and Renaissance-inspired arches and columns, now stands in solitary splendour between the park and the formal terraces round the house. The park is a largely seventeenth-century creation but the terraces were laid out by Thomas James Agar, later created Baron Robartes of Lanhydrock (the previous title having lapsed in 1764) in the mid-nineteenth century. Stately rows of cone-shaped Irish yews flank the terrace immediately in front of the house, while the slightly lower terraces are enclosed either by a castellated stone wall or by low box hedges. Within these confines geometrically patterned flowerbeds planted mainly with roses break up the smooth grass parterres. The magnificent bronze urns, decorated in the Baroque manner with cherubs, heavy swags of fruit, animal masks, and vines in high relief, are thought to be the work of Louis XIV's goldsmith Louis Ballin. The fashionable London architect George Gilbert Scott advised Lord Robartes on the lay-out of these elaborate terraces and also enlarged the house, adding a coach-house and stables to the south-east.

On a stormy day in April 1881 the kitchen chimney caught fire. The flames quickly spread and gutted the entire house apart from the north wing and the entrance porch. The Robartes were rescued but Lady Robartes died a few days afterwards from shock. Bereft at the loss of his wife and his house, Lord Robartes fell into a decline and died the following year. Happily, their son Thomas Charles rebuilt Lanhydrock in the original manner.

Inside, to comply with the Victorian demand for comfort, an underground boiler house was installed to heat water (a reservoir filled from a nearby source was built on top of the hill behind the house and provided a constant supply) for household use. The boiler also fed hot water to a network of radiators, some of which are superb specimens with oak cases and marble tops. Electric lighting was put in, and the lay-out of the interior radically altered, particularly with regard to the servants' quarters. As Mark Girouard points out in his *Life in the English Country House*, the Victorians did not necessarily employ more servants than before, but their accommodation changed 'to make them more moral and more efficient'. In the name of morality men and women were kept apart at all times, except when under supervision. Nothing was left to chance. The attic bedrooms for the male and female servants at Lanhydrock are reached by separate staircases. The servants were reminded of their moral duty when they assembled with the family for prayers in the prayer room. There was little opportunity for even a brief encounter with the opposite sex during working hours. The butler's premises were in one part of the house, the housekeeper's in another. The footmen and housemaids worked, as it were, in different domains and would only meet at mealtimes in the servants' hall.

hydrock kitchen,
wing the spit.

hydrock.
ly Robartes'
ice.

Photo, A. F. Kersting. By kind permission of the National Trust.

Lanhydrock. The Jacobean Long Gallery soon after the house was given to the National Trust in 1953.

Lanhydrock. The ceiling of the Long Gallery: detail of the plasterwork, showing Adam and Eve in the Ga▶

Photo, A. F. Kersting. By kind permission of the National Trust.

No expense was spared in the building of new kitchen quarters in the south-west corner of the house. A scullery, a dairy, three larders for meat, fish and groceries, and a bakehouse are grouped round an enormous kitchen. Clerestory windows high up in the roof (they are opened by ingenious mechanisms on the end wall) as well as large windows below ensure not only a light kitchen but a fresh-smelling one. As a further precaution, fumes from the huge coal fire could escape through metal grids in the wall above. Food was kept hot in a serving-room next to the dining-room. The dishes were placed in the massive iron cupboard heated by hot water pipes which is still there today.

The Victorians had a passion for segregation. To judge from the number of backstairs and back corridors at Lanhydrock, the staff could go about their business without bumping into members of the family. They were not to be seen and not to be heard, rather like the children, who, of course, were banished to the nursery wing. Even Lord and Lady Robartes had their own demarcation lines. The oak-panelled billiard room and smoking room on the ground floor were a strictly male preserve where the men would gather after dinner. They are hung predictably with old photographs of school and college teams and with engravings of Lord's cricket ground. On the first floor, well away from the men's social gatherings, is Lady Robartes' suite of rooms, comfortably furnished with buttonback chairs, William Morris wallpaper and much cheerful bric à brac. If her boudoir symbolises Victorian cosiness and clutter, the large drawing-room nearby, whose furniture is in fact largely Georgian, represents Victorian formality.

A small flight of steps at the end of the drawing-room leads into the enormous Jacobean gallery that survived the fire. It is 116 feet long and runs the length of the north wing. The plasterwork of the magnificent barrel-vaulted ceiling is well worth a close look. The main panels, twenty-four in all, are star-shaped and depict in lively fashion various Old Testament subjects. Smaller panels portray a wonderful array of birds and beasts, some real, some imaginary. But when viewed as a whole, it is the amazingly intricate pattern of strapwork that catches the eye. Whoever the plasterers may have been (the National Trust attributes this ceiling and the one at Prideaux Place 'almost certainly' to a Devonshire family of plasterers, the Abbots of Frithelstock near Bideford), they had a superb sense of design as well as imagination.

The higher garden, behind the house and little church, makes a good starting-point for a tour of the garden and the vast park, which was laid out in 1860 at the same time as the terraces, by Thomas James Agar. Many of the original flowerbeds on the lower slopes have disappeared and the flowering shrubs (the usual mixture of magnolias, azaleas and rhododendrons) are largely twentieth-century additions. A curious assortment of buildings provides support for many of the plants. Flowering quinces, firethorn, and a trumpet vine grow up the wall of a picturesque thatched cottage. Nearby is a small, partly sunken edifice whose quaint gables end in tight twirls, like a roll of granite carpet, marking the site of the Holy Well used by the monks of St Petroc long, long ago.

A wide, winding path leads from the Higher Garden up the hill behind the house. Clusters of many coloured rhododendrons grow on the grassy slopes, together with specimen trees, and a pink magnolia forms an archway over the path itself. Graceful beech trees crown the summit, and while enjoying their shade you can look down, past the kaleidoscopic colours of the Higher Garden, to the solitary gatehouse and the great avenue of sycamores beyond. These were planted in 1648 by the 2nd Lord Robartes, and in the nineteenth century a row of beeches was planted next to them, so that the approach to the house would still be lined with trees when the sycamores died. A small gateway marks the entrance to the Great Wood, which offers a number of different routes back to the house. Giant-leaved Himalayan rhododendrons and plantations of azaleas greet the eye, as well as thousands of bluebells.

Thomas Charles Robartes, who rebuilt Lanhydrock after the fire, succeeded to the Viscountcy of Clifden in 1899. His eldest son, Tommy Agar-Robartes, was a prominent Cornish Liberal and much loved in the county. As an officer in the Guards he died gallantly on the Western Front in the First World War, attempting to save the life of a wounded comrade, for which action he was recommended for a posthumous VC. There is a moving memorial to him in Truro Cathedral. The second son, Francis Gerald, became the 7th Viscount. Francis never married and neither did his two sisters. They lived together at Lanhydrock for over thirty years and gave the house and park to the National Trust in 1953. It is to be hoped that the monks of St Petroc would have approved of the pleasure Lanhydrock gives to so many today.

7.
Powder

The whole castle beginneth to mourne, and to wringe out harde stones
for teares, that shee that was imbraced, visited and delighted with greate
princes, is now desolate, forsaken, and forlorne.

John Norden, *Description of Cornwall*, 1610

RESTORMEL CASTLE, so poignantly described by Norden, lies in the north-east
corner of Powder Hundred about a mile to the north of the old town of
Lostwithiel. In the Middle Ages the river Fowey was still navigable at this point,
and Lostwithiel was an important trading centre. It is thought that the Norman
lord, Baldwin Fitz Turstin, who held many manors for Count Robert of
Mortain, bridged the river Fowey in about 1100 and built a fort high above it to
protect the new crossing. Turstin's domain was worth guarding, for the weekly
markets at Lostwithiel meant that handsome sums of money, tolls for the right
to trade and rents from each stall holder, went into the owner's pocket. Richard,
Earl of Cornwall, naturally wished to gain control of such a valuable asset. He
had already secured Launceston and Tintagel and in 1270 he persuaded Isolda de
Cardinan to sell him her Restormel estates and the borough of Lostwithiel.

Restormel was the favourite residence of Richard's son Edmund, the next Earl
of Cornwall, and it was he who decided to make Lostwithiel his seat of
government in the county. Edmund constructed a splendid range of buildings for
his new centre of administration. There was a hall of the exchequer for the
payment of dues; a coinage hall where a coign or corner was cut from each tin
lode for assay; a stannary hall for the evaluation of tin and a stannary court
where the disputes and debts of the tinners were settled. Fragments of these old
buildings can still be seen in some of the houses in the town.

In the Middle Ages Restormel Castle stood in a vast deer park. Nothing
remains of Baldwin Fitz Turstin's castle except some early masonry at the base
of the gate tower. The circular wall of the shell keep was erected about a hundred
years later, at the end of the twelfth century. Built of local slate with dressings
of white Pentewan stone, it is well protected by a deep flat-bottomed ditch below
and by a battlemented parapet round the eight-foot-wide wall-walk above. This
was the castle which Richard bought from Isolda de Cardinan and which his son
Edmund enlarged and refined.

Inside the keep, Edmund erected a series of rooms for his personal use. The
partition walls survive today, so that it is possible to visualise those luxurious
new living quarters. To the right of the gate is the kitchen, the only room which
rises to the full height of the castle. The colossal fireplace built into the curtain

wall, as well as the adjoining buttery and pantry, are evidence of the Earl's hospitality. All the other rooms at ground floor level served as storerooms and have low ceilings. The principal rooms — the great hall, the solar, the ante-chapel and two bedchambers, as one proceeds in an anti-clockwise direction — were built above these storerooms, away from the courtyard bustle and with easy access to the wall-walk. Large windows cut through the curtain wall gave each room a wide view over the hills and woods of the surrounding countryside; log fires would have provided warmth and a flickering light as darkness fell.

The bailey or outer court on the west flank of the hill comprised servants' quarters, stables, offices, storerooms, and a chapel. From the higher ground above the bailey, water from various springs was channelled through a leaden conduit into the moat and keep. A deep well in the courtyard inside the keep, the original water supply of the castle, was retained for use in an emergency, should the conduit be damaged during an attack.

After Edmund's death in 1299 Restormel was virtually unused. The Black Prince visited the castle in 1354 and 1365, in search, one suspects, of money rather than of pleasure. He wished to collect his feudal dues and to raise money and troops before setting off for Bordeaux, where he maintained the most glittering court in Europe. Like the other strongholds in his Duchy, Restormel deteriorated; although briefly held by Lord Essex for Parliament during the Civil War it was never used again.

BOUND by Falmouth estuary to the west and by Fowey estuary to the east, Powder Hundred's coast is well protected by **St Mawes Castle** and **St Catherine's Castle**, which guard the approaches to these two great rivers. Both were built by Henry VIII in the late 1530s and 1540s as part of his defence of the realm.※

Earlier in his reign Henry had built small blockhouses at St Mawes to stop enemy and pirate ships from entering the river Fal, but he now ordered a fortress to be built close to the water. Thomas Treffry, Clerk of Works to the King, was in charge of the operation, and a military architect from Moravia, Stefan von Haschenperg, is known to have been employed by Henry in the 1530s. His ideas were brought into play at St Mawes. Work began in 1540. The design of the castle was unlike anything the English had seen before. The invention of cannon and gunpowder had rendered tall keeps and gatehouses obsolete. Nor was St Mawes ever intended as a nobleman's residence, as most mediæval castles were. Three low, semi-circular bastions surround the central tower, which served as a garrison for as many as a hundred men. The mess-room was on the ground floor, and the kitchen in the basement. Large cannon were placed in the courtyards of the bastions, and light guns in the embrasures on the rampart walls. There are eight further recesses for gunners in the upper room of the tower. Entrance to the castle was via a drawbridge on the landward side. Latin inscriptions singing

Restormel Castle (late 12th century), Lostwithiel.

Fowey Haven. Part of a chart drawn in the reign of Henry VIII showing St Catherine's Castle at the harbour entrance, the toll or south gate of Fowey and, next to the church, the battlemented walls of Place.

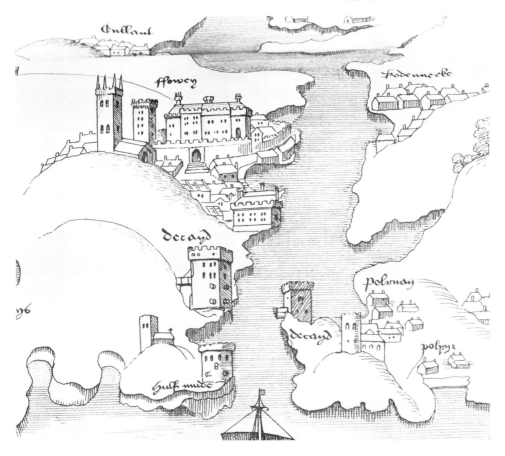

the King's praises appear on the walls of the keep, as well as lively gargoyles and an elaborate royal coat of arms.

Michael Vyvyan of Trelowarren became governor of St Mawes Castle in 1544. This was an onerous task since he was required to maintain the garrison at his own expense. Nearly a hundred years later this unrewarding position proved too much for his descendant Sir Francis Vyvyan, governor in the early seventeenth century. He was dismissed in 1632, and it was left to his successor, Hannibal Bonython, to rescue St Mawes from dire poverty. Fourteen years later he surrendered the castle to Fairfax's Parliamentary force without a fight. He can hardly be blamed, for the garrison was poorly equipped for a siege without arms or sufficient ammunition. This inglorious action was the castle's first and last.

Fowey, with its maze of tiny streets rising steeply from the huge natural harbour, was always prone to attack by virtue of its importance as a port and a haven for shipping. During the fifteenth century the town thrived on privateering and piracy. The renowned 'Fowey gallants' used to attack French ships off the Breton coast and strip them of their cargoes. Reprisals were inevitable: in 1457 French pirate ships sailed into the harbour under cover of darkness. The inhabitants rallied to the town's defence under the direction of Elizabeth Treffry of Place, whose house afforded them a degree of safety as the marauding French set fire to the houses below. Having learned a bitter lesson, the men of Fowey constructed two blockhouses on either side of the mouth of the river and suspended a heavy chain between the two as a way of at least damaging enemy vessels. A century later Henry VIII erected St Catherine's Castle on the south side of the harbour as a precaution against intruders.

Of simpler construction than St Mawes Castle, it consists of a single round tower, which housed six cannon. It is best seen from the other side of the water at Polruan.

PLACE, still the seat of the ancient Treffry family whose history is inextricably linked with that of Fowey, is scarcely visible from the town or the waterfront. Its battlemented walls appear to circumscribe the town rather than a particular house. The Treffry family was well established there by the late Middle Ages.*

John Leland, Henry VIII's antiquarian and chaplain, stayed at Place in 1538, perhaps in order to keep an eye on Thomas Treffry as he oversaw the construction of the coastline defences already mentioned. He commented that an earlier Thomas Treffry, husband of the redoubtable Elizabeth who had repulsed the French, 'builded a righte fair and stronge embatelid tower in his house and embatteling all the walles of the house in a manner made it a castelle'. This description matches a drawing of Place, made on a contemporary map, which shows a house with a tower surrounded by a high battlemented wall.**

Joseph Thomas Austen, who inherited the property through his mother in 1786, rebuilt Place between 1813 and 1845. Romantic on the one hand,

Place, Fowey. 19th-century engraving of the south front with the library and drawing-room bow.

traditionalist on the other, he chose the Regency Gothic style as a way of remaining faithful to the mediæval Gothic of the original house, much of which remains. The Tudor courtyard, with its handsome oriel window, is still the centre of Place, although the rooms around it were rearranged. The hall became the dining-room, the solar became the library. Very sensibly, Joseph Thomas Treffry — he assumed the name when High Sheriff in 1838 — restored the magnificent oak-beamed ceiling of the hall and preserved the mid-eighteenth century ceiling in the library. The beautiful rococo plasterwork of the latter was executed by Mr Heyden and Mr Lorington who had been working at Carclew for the Truro mining magnate William Lemon. The Regency Gothic bay window in the library, with its decorative tracery, was inspired by the Tudor bay window of the morning room. In such thoughtful ways were past and present linked. Lastly, Mr Treffry added the granite towers, thus maintaining the fortified appearance of old Place. The entrance hall was built entirely of porphyry from his own quarries.

The gardens at Place were redesigned in about 1900 by the landscape gardener T. H. Mawson. Captivated by the natural beauty of the site, Mawson created a series of terraces and walks running parallel to, but high above, the river. These flanked one side of the long carriage drive. Overgrown long since, it is the present owner's wish to recreate them in part.

IF the remodelling of Place allowed the remarkably intelligent and resourceful Mr J. T. Treffry to indulge his fancy, his other activities reveal an intensely practical side to his character. With great energy and enterprise, he became the largest employer of labour in the Westcountry, owning mines, granite quarries and railways. He also built Par harbour and the present main road into Fowey. He was deeply concerned with the early development of railways in Cornwall and constructed the line from Par to Newquay. As the first Chairman of the Cornwall Railway, he was closely associated with the engineer I. K. Brunel in the project for building the great railway bridge across the Tamar, although this was not completed until after his death. Perhaps Joseph Thomas Treffry is best remembered for the construction of the **Treffry Viaduct** across the deep Luxulyan valley to the north-west of Fowey, its purpose being to carry water and a light railway, now disused. This colossal granite structure, nearly 700 feet long and 700 feet high with 10 gigantic arches, is a tribute to its creator.

COMPARED to the Treffrys, the Rashleighs were newcomers when, as ambitious Devon merchants, they came to trade in Fowey in the sixteenth century. In 1545 Philip Rashleigh bought the manor of **Trenant**, just a few miles to the west of Fowey. It originally belonged to the priory of Tywardreath, but after the Dissolution monastic lands were sold off in order to raise money for Henry VIII's disastrous wars. Philip was quick to seize this golden opportunity to acquire land, and his son John added to the estates by buying Bodmin Priory in 1567. Although a furnished chamber was kept clean and aired for his use, he never made the priory a permanent home. It was divided up into separate tenements and soon fell into a state of disrepair.

JOHN RASHLEIGH decided early in his career to make Fowey his base, and his town house, now the **Ship Hotel** at the bottom of Lostwithiel Street, looked on to what is now called Trafalgar Square. John and his wife Alice renovated the house in 1570 and the oak-panelled room with their names carved on the mantel has been preserved. Caryatids and other Renaissance motifs show local awareness of Italianate ideas. A doorway that still exists in the upper storey used to lead into a room in the arch across Lostwithiel Street. This was the toll gate or south gate of the town, pulled down in 1876. The existing front of the Ship Inn is late nineteenth century.

IN about 1600 John built himself a fine new mansion on the land he had acquired between Fowey and Gribbin Head. **Menabilly**, now the home of the Rashleigh family, was entirely rebuilt in the early eighteenth century and substantially altered in the 1820s when the grounds were landscaped. Sheltered by woodland and stretching down to a secluded bay, these were planted with sub-tropical plants and rare shrubs.

For many years Menabilly was the home of the writer Dame Daphne du Maurier and her husband, General Sir Frederick Browning. Its secluded atmosphere must have contributed to the character of Manderley in her celebrated novel, *Rebecca*; and Menabilly is at the centre of her less well-known but outstanding novel of the Civil War, *The King's General*.

HELIGAN House stands at the head of a valley overlooking the fishing harbour of Mevagissey. Home to the Tremayne family since about 1603, the house fell into serious decline after the First and Second World Wars and was finally sold and converted into flats in 1970. Sadly, the original brick façade has now been white-washed. The gardens, however, thanks to an ambitious and inspired restoration scheme begun in 1991, are now an outstanding testament to every aspect of nineteenth-century horticulture.

The re-awakening of these lost gardens, found slumbering beneath an impenetrable tangle of bramble and laurel, catches the imagination of all who visit them. Once the site was cleared — a Herculean task involving the felling of hundreds of trees that had crashed to the ground during the 1990 hurricane — plant material of dazzling size and beauty began to emerge. Among the most exciting finds were gigantic rhododendrons introduced by Sir Joseph Hooker from his 1847-51 plant collecting expeditions in the Sikkim Himalayas. Clustered round a lawn, now known as Flora's Green, are marvellous examples of *R. thomsonii* with its blood-red flowers and cinnamon bark and the creamy, purple-blotched *R. falconeri*. An even earlier introduction is the *Cornus capitata* which arrived at Heligan in the 1820s and once lined the long drive. A new avenue has been planted and in the years to come will look resplendent when each tree bears its sulphur-yellow bracts in summer, followed by large strawberry-like fruits in autumn.

More interesting specimen trees were discovered in the aptly named 'Jungle' garden, a steep-sided valley with four interconnecting ponds. The exuberant growth is overwhelming. Huge conifers from Japan (*Pinus thunbergii*) and New Zealand (*Podocarpus totara*) tower above this luscious ravine and protect the palms and tree ferns beneath.

The gardens not only celebrate the achievements of the plant collectors but also the skills of the Victorian head gardener whose triumphs were largely brought about under glass. The walled gardens were his domain and there are four at Heligan. The kitchen garden now grows almost two acres of vegetables using traditional methods. Victorian varieties are tried and tasted, the aim being to discover the best flavour of each type. The sight of the asparagus beds, the seedling lettuces and rows of curly kale, sea kale and kohl rabi, so rarely seen or eaten now, is mouth-watering. Espaliered apple trees have been trained over arches and the entire length of the lavender edged paths.

Likewise cordons of pears, apricots, cherries and plums brighten the curved south-facing wall of the adjacent walled area known as the Melon Yard. Here melons and cucumbers were carefully nurtured in glasshouses first heated by fermenting manure and then, in the 1860s, by boiler heating from the stovehouse behind. Pineapples were even more prized. These were grown in pots which were plunged up to their rims in moist, fermenting tanner's bark laid down in pits with brick sides and a glass roof. Running the entire length of the pit to the front and rear were trenches filled with fresh manure. Heat from decomposition passed through the brick walls through square pigeon holes, ensuring a temperature of about 120°C for the pineapples. Even so, it took eighteen months to grow a mature pineapple and a further six months to ripen it. Today Queen and Cayenne pineapples from Natal are now growing in the pits.

Beyond the Melon Yard is the Flower Garden, its gently sloping beds now divided into neat rows of summer vegetables — lettuces, radishes and beetroot to name only a few — and flowers to be cut for the house. Here the list is endless: larkspur, asters, alstroemerias, white chrysanthemums, iris, sweet william, scabious and cornflowers. Sweet peas clamber up and through sprays of beechwood planted in double rows or, wigwam like, in small circles. Handsome glasshouses now stand restored along the south facing wall. The citrus house, complete with brick terrace upon which stood the citrus plants in the summer, dates from the 1840s, while the vinery alongside is now a fine example of a fruit house designed by Sir Joseph Paxton for the mass market in about 1850. On the west-facing wall is a large unheated peach house, now containing peaches, guavas and passion fruits.

Team work at Heligan exemplifies Victorian efficiency and pride, as well as confidence in the future. The recreation of a 300 foot long herbaceous border is next on the agenda.

TREWITHEN, mid-way between St Austell and Truro in the parish of Probus, must take pride of place as the finest eighteenth-century house in Powder. Building began not long after Philip Hawkins, a wealthy attorney's son, bought the estate in 1715. The Cornish historian Thomas Tonkin noted, in the *Parochial History* that he began in 1702, that Trewithen Barton had previously belonged to the Williams family but that Courtenay Williams had foolishly squandered away 'a pretty estate and a good fortune too', and sold the barton to Philip Hawkins. Philip thereupon 'very much improved this seat, new built a great part of the house, made good gardens etc.'*

The north or entrance front of Trewithen, with its recessed centre, is built of bricks made from blue clay dug on the estate. The porosity of the bricks meant that after a period of weathering the brickwork had to be sealed. In 1948 the north front was therefore re-rendered with a special concrete mixture (the sand came from Hayle Towans, owned by the Hawkins in the eighteenth century), which happened to have the same ingredients as Pentewan granite. As a result, the concrete facing blends perfectly with the other three sides of the house which are built of solid Pentewan stone. This stone is a soft silvery grey on a dry day, but when the air is laden with moisture it has a definite pinkish hue. Sombre granite keystones above each sash window are the only decorative feature of the otherwise plain north front, but its severity is subtly tempered by the presence of two detached wings of pinky red bricks surmounted by matching cupolas, one of which contains the oldest single-handed clock in Cornwall. These attractive buildings stand at right angles to the house and frame the forecourt in a firm but casual way. The east wing was originally a stable block, while the west wing contained a laundry and bakehouse, the estate office, and a court room where the annual rent dinner was held.

Philip Hawkins had no children and his cousin Thomas succeeded to the estate in 1738. The south or garden front was probably built in his time and is thought to be the work of the architect Sir Robert Taylor, possibly following Thomas Edwards' design. It is grander than its north-facing counterpart.

The central block projects rather than recedes in a gesture of assertion. Its elegance is due to the strong but simple stone cornice and the delicately carved consoles beneath the window frames. The central window on the ground floor is further stressed by the addition of an imposing entablature supported by similar but larger, consoles.

A magnificent dining-room fills the five central bays of the south front, its rococo stucco decoration indicating a mid-eighteenth century date. Graceful garlands and floral pendants beneath candle brackets break up the wall space, painted a soft Wedgwood green, while the length of the room is relieved by triple arches at either end which form a vaulted arcade. Each arch is supported by Ionic columns matched by Ionic pilasters on the wall which offset the various portraits. Two of the finest, by Sir Joshua Reynolds, are of Dr Zachariah Mudge and his wife. Mrs Mudge, it will be remembered, severely scolded Dr Johnson for drinking his seventeenth cup of tea. The Mudges became associated with Trewithen by marriage, and another Reynolds portrait of Kitty Mudge, as the Market Girl, hangs in the drawing-room. There are also four fine portraits of the Hawkins family by Allan Ramsay, an unusual choice of artist in Cornwall.

Thomas Hawkins married Ann Heywood, the daughter of a well-to-do London cloth merchant. Her sophisticated taste and fashion consciousness are reflected in the elegant interior of Trewithen. As a young bride she would have supervised the decoration of the dining-room and drawing-room, the one in the rococo manner, the other with Chinese Chippendale fretwork over the handsome doorways. The craftsmanship is superb, whatever the detailing. Ann was a perfectionist for whom nothing but the best would suffice.

If Ann's taste is manifest inside Trewithen, Thomas's influence lives on outside. He was responsible for the two detached wings and for landscaping the garden. An engraving in Borlase's *Natural History of Cornwall* shows the garden as it was in his time. Rows of beech hedges flank each side of the south front to create a formal vista and to protect the house from the prevailing wind. Avenues radiate from the house to the east and to the north, with a landscaped park beyond. But Thomas did not live to see his trees mature. Having set an example to the wary villagers by having himself vaccinated against smallpox, he died of the disease in 1766, at the age of only forty-two. His eldest son Christopher, created a baronet in 1799, inherited Trewithen and greatly increased the family's fortunes.*

Christopher's nephew, Christopher Henry Thomas Hawkins, succeeded him in 1829. He was the last Hawkins to inhabit Trewithen, for on his death in 1903 the estate passed, through his sister Mary Ann, to the Johnstone family. George H. Johnstone, grandfather of the present owner, was largely responsible for the magnificent gardens we see today. When he inherited the estate in 1904, Thomas Hawkins' beech hedges were mature trees. Three hundred of these were felled by government order during the First World War, which meant that openings were made in the wood on each side of the south front. These empty spaces cried out to be filled, and George Johnstone was convinced that the more tender species of rhododendron, camellia and magnolia would flourish in such a sheltered environment. Trewithen today leaves us in no doubt that he was right. It was the beginning of a golden age of planting.

The setting for a vast carpet of lawn, over two hundred metres long, which rolls away from the south front towards a woodland shrubbery is George Johnstone's greatest achievement. This immense glade is lined on both sides by a dazzling range of trees and shrubs, many of which were raised from seed collected in the wild by the great pioneer plant collectors at the turn of the century. Magnolias came from E. H. Wilson's expedition to China in 1899, camellias from George Forrest's Himalayan expedition, and rhododendrons from Kingdon Ward's explorations in Assam and Burma. Among the most beautiful are the white *Magnolia mollicomata*, now a tall tree; *Magnolia campbellii* with deeper pink flowers; the famous brilliant yellow *Rhododendron macabeanum*, collected in Manipur by Kingdon Ward, and the white or pinkish *Camellia saluenensis*, brought back by Forrest.

George Johnstone not only introduced these exotic plants to Trewithen but raised many hybrids himself, some of which are named, endearingly, after those close to him. *R* 'Alison Johnstone' is named after his wife, *R*. 'Jack Skilton' after his head gardener and *C*. 'Elizabeth Johnstone' after one of his daughters. He also bred an astonishing variety of daffodils. The yellows range from palest primrose to Van Gogh gold, but there are whity pinks, creamy whites and even tinges of blue to be seen at close range.

This passionate plantsman loved to experiment, as a painter does, with form and colour. Like any artist concerned with visual beauty, he aspired to create a unified, balanced composition. Great care and thought have gone into the design of the gardens. Each area is different, yet related to the whole. To the east of the great glade is a path leading to an avenue of sycamores which commands a fine

Trewithen. The south front.

Trewithen, Probus. Engraving from Borlase's Natural History of Cornwall (1758) showing the rows of beech trees planted by Thomas Hawkins on either side of the south front in the mid-18th century.

view across the park. Beside the path is a row of specimens of two very primitive trees, *Metasequoia glyptostroboides* or Dawn Redwood and *Ginkgo biloba* or Maidenhair tree. A male specimen of the latter was planted at Kew in 1762 and is there to this day. The branch of a female grafted on to it in 1911 produced seeds eight years later. The Trewithen ginkgos were planted soon afterwards.

To the west of the glade is the camellia walk. Here are magnificent examples of *C. saluenensis* and *C. reticulata forma simplex* grown from Chinese seed, successful clones such as *C.* 'Trewithen Pink', *C.* 'Trewithen Salmon', *C.* 'Elizabeth Johnstone' and many forms of *C. x williamsii*, to be mentioned later in connection with Caerhays. Dwarf rhododendrons planted alongside the camellias burst into bloom in May. The camellia walk leads to the Cock Pit, a deep dell filled with rhododendrons and primulas as well as tree ferns from New Zealand, a Japanese maple and large pink *Magnolia sprengeri*.

In contrast to this exotic underworld full of riotous colour, the small walled garden that fills the angle between house and stable block on the west side is of a quieter beauty. Formality and intimacy come as a relief after the riotous planting 'in the wild'. A slightly sunken ornamental pond at one end is complemented at the other end by a raised terrace complete with summerhouse and rose trellis. More roses fill the flowerbeds which break up the rectangular grass parterre in the centre. This is surrounded by a path of granite sets from the old Camborne-Redruth tramway, lovingly laid out by George Johnstone himself. Quintessentially English borders packed with pinks, lupins, michaelmas daisies, and delphiniums in high summer flank the long sides of the rectangle and make a contrast to shrubs.

No great garden ever stands still. Having lost many of the old beech trees in the past decade, the present owners have created an arboretum to provide the necessary shelter in the years ahead. Pines and eucalyptus from all over the world have been collected and planting still continues. Public money has been made available through grants to help repair the damage done by the great storm of 1990 and to restore the park to the original landscape plan drawn up in 1735 and still in the family's possession.

TREGREHAN GARDEN, two miles outside St Austell on the way to St Blazey, is one of the most romantic and atmospheric gardens in Cornwall. A magnificent avenue of limes flanks the foot of the drive which then sweeps in an upward curve through parkland to the house. The Carlyon family has lived at Tregrehan since 1565 and the present house (not open to the public) was built in 1680, enlarged in the 1770s and again in 1848.

Throughout the nineteenth century the Carlyons were enthralled by the range of new and beautiful trees — conifers in particular — that were being brought back by plant collectors such as David Douglas and William Lobb from the West coast of America and South America and by others from Japan. Little by little they planted the sheltered slopes and floor of a north-south running valley to one side of the house. Protected from frost and wind, many of these conifers have reached an exceptional height and size and are among the finest specimens in this country. Most notable are *Tsuga dumosa* and *Cedrus deodara* from the Himalayas, *Tsuga heterophylla*, *Thuja plicata*, *Sequoiadendron giganteum*, *Picea sitchensis* and *Pseudotsuga menziesii* from North America and *Thuja standishii* and *Cryptomeria japonica* from Japan. These conifers are interplanted with ornamental evergreen beeches from New Zealand such as *Nothofagus fusca*, *Nothofagus menziesii* and *Nothofagus solandri*. Near the stream at the bottom of the valley is a huge *Gingko biloba*, its leaves turning to a beautiful clear yellow before falling in autumn. Commonly planted in the vicinity of Buddhist temples in the East, this sacred tree has thrived in the peace and solitude of this magical wood. High above, near the house, a solemn avenue of ancient yew trees has intertwined in a pointed arch over a long, straight path, soaring upwards like the nave of a cathedral.

Tregrehan is also famous for its rhododendrons and camellias. There are fine specimens of *R. hookeri*, *falconeri*, *griffithianum* and *grande* behind the sunken garden, while some of the earliest camellias planted in the garden are to be found outside the walled garden, These include the species *C. saluenensis*, *cuspidata*, *sinensis* and *maliflora*. In the 1970s and 1980s Miss Gillian Carlyon raised a number of interesting and beautiful hybrids such as the semi-double pale silvery pink *Jenefer Carlyon*, the rose madder paeony-like *Tristrem Carlyon* and the semi-double dog rose pink *Marjorie Waldegrave*, named after her mother. A large range of the Carlyon hybrids are now available in the nursery.

The mid-nineteenth century glasshouses at the top end of the walled garden have recently been restored and contain many sub-tropical species although the greenhouses are not heated. These include tender plants of many genera seen in the woodland, such as the rhododendron, camellia and hydrangea. *Passiflora*, *Myosotidium* (the vivid blue Chatham Island forget-me-not) and a range of *Lapageria* colour forms all thrive in this frost-free environment.

Tregrehan garden proves beyond any doubt the suitability of the Cornish climate to grow rare Temperate Rainforest trees. Since many of these forests in the Southern Hemisphere are threatened with extinction due to the high commercial value of the timber and the slow regeneration rate of the trees, their survival at Tregrehan makes the garden an important botanical resource. Since the current owner was born in New Zealand, he is determined that planting and conservation shall continue. On the other side of the stream at the bottom of the valley he has begun to plant trees from New Zealand, Australia and South America. In years to come this will be as outstanding an arboretum as his forebears planted over a hundred years ago.

THREE great nineteenth-century mansions in Powder — Tregothnan, Trelissick, and Caerhays — are the visible expression of the vast fortunes made by managers and landowners alike from the Cornish tin and copper mines.*

Foremost among these families were the Boscawens of **Tregothnan**. Their huge house stands on a hill above the east bank of Tresillian river, a tidal creek that joins the Truro river and then flows into the Fal. Tregothnan means 'the house at the head of the valley' and is the seat of Lord Falmouth today.

The Boscawens originally lived at Boscawen Ros in the parish of St Buryan, near Land's End, but when John de Boscawen married the heiress Joan de Tregothnan in 1335, he moved to Tregothnan where his descendants have continued to live. The original Tudor house, a two-storied building with a battlemented tower and arched doorway beneath, lay to the north-west of the present terrace where a number of ilexes grow. All that remains is the old doorway which stands at the entrance to the kitchen garden.

In the 1650s Hugh Boscawen built a fine new house which his cousin Celia Fiennes (Hugh's first wife was Margaret Fiennes, daughter of the Earl of Lincoln) describes in her journal of 1698 when she travelled to Land's End on horseback. How glad she must have been to be 'civilly entertained' by her relatives after riding in wet weather along rough roads. 'The house', she noted, 'is built of white stone like the rough coarse marble [Truro porphyry] and covered with slate; they use much lime in their cement which makes both walls and cover look very white.' It was a rectangular block with a hipped roof, typical of a type of house built during the Commonwealth and which Sir John Summerson refers to as 'artisan mannerist' in style.

The entrance, [Celia goes on] is up a few stone steps into a large high hall and so to a passage that leads foreright up a good staircase; on the right side is a large common little parlour for constant eating in, from whence goes a little room for smoking that has a back way into the kitchen and on the left hand is a great parlour and drawing-roome wainscoted all very well, but plaine.

Hugh Boscawen's nephew inherited Tregothnan and was created Viscount Falmouth in 1720 for his services to George I as Controller of the Household. His son John married Joan Blanchland, who brought with her a large estate on the opposite side of the Fal. Soon afterwards rich lodes of copper were found on this land and successfully mined, thereby greatly increasing the Boscawen fortune. The 4th Viscount Falmouth, created 1st Earl of Falmouth at George IV's coronation, employed William Wilkins, architect of the National Gallery in Trafalgar Square, to enlarge Tregothnan in the 1820s. Wilkins turned the sober seventeenth-century house into a picturesque 'Tudor' castle. An imposing three-sided 'gatehouse' acts as a huge covered entrance porch in the middle of the north front, its Gothic windows and arches an effective contrast to the square mullioned and transomed windows on either side. The curiously shaped pinnacles on top of the angle turrets are replicas of the pinnacles of East Barsham Manor, a late tudor house in Norfolk. In 1845, another architect called Vulliamy enlarged the south front for the 2nd Earl, adding a gabled wing and towers at the west end.

When Celia Fiennes visited Tregothnan the garden was hardly established. It had 'gravel walks round and across', she recorded, 'but the squares are full of gooseberry and shrub trees and look more like a kitchen garden as Lady Mary Boscawen told me, out of which is another garden and orchard which is something like a grove, green walks with rows of fruit trees; it is capable of being a fine place with some charge . . .'

Evelyn Boscawen, the 6th Viscount Falmouth, was largely responsible for the layout of the present gardens which cover an area of about forty acres. In the 1850s and 1860s he and his brother John, the Rector of nearby Lamorran, planted many varieties of *Camellia japonica* near the east front of the house. These were removed to the far end of the garden soon after 1897 where they now flourish at the top of a slope known as Snowdrop Hill. They include 'Lady de Saumarez', 'Wilbankiana', 'Arejishi', 'Hornsby Pink', 'Canon Boscawen', 'Tricolor' and 'Imbricata Alba'. Apart from 'Lady Clare' and 'Nagasaki', no new plantings of the modern camellia varieties were made until 1956 when C. 'Magnolia flora', 'Salutation', 'J. C. Williams' and 'Donation' were planted. In recent years new varieties have been planted including 'Drama Girl', 'Prince Albert', 'Apple Blossom' and 'Golden Spangles'.

In front of the summer house is a large expanse of grass flanked by vast clumps of blood-red *Rhododendron arboreum*. Well over one hundred years old, these are now almost fifty feet high. Other rhododendrons include a number discovered by Joseph Hooker in 1848 and described in his book *The Rhododendrons of the Sikkim-Himalayas*. Two of the most beautiful are *R. falconeri*, a tree with creamy bell-like flowers marked with purple in the throat found near Darjeeling, and the beautiful yellow *R. campylocarpum* from Sikkim.

THOMAS DANIELL began his career as clerk to the Truro mining magnate William Lemon, but later made a fortune in his own right. In the 1750s he employed the architect of Trewithen, Thomas Edwards, to build the **Mansion House** in Truro. His wife's uncle, Ralph Allen of Bath, made them a gift of stone from his own quarries to build the new house. Delivered by barge to Daniell's quay on the river at the bottom of the garden, it launched an immediate vogue for Bath stone, which was subsequently used for houses in nearby Lemon Street.

IN 1800 Thomas Daniell's son, Ralph Allen, acquired **Trelissick**, a modest mid-eighteenth century house designed by Sir Humphrey Davey's grandfather for a captain in the county militia. Ralph Allen's son, Thomas, rebuilt the house in 1825, adding an imposing but austere neo-classical shell to the existing core. He

Mansion House, Truro. Designed by Thomas Edwards for Thomas Daniell c. 1750.

Trelissick, near Truro. Remodelled by P. F.Robinson, a pupil of Henry Holland, in 1825 for the Daniell family.

Photo, A. F. Kersting. By kind permission of the National Trust.

Tree fern *Dicksonia antarctica*.

Magnolia campbellii 'Lanarth'.

Rhododendron macabeanum.

Pieris formosa forrestii and *Pieris* 'Forest Flame'.

Trewithen. pp. 92-94

Tregrehan garden in spring.
Trelissick garden. Azaleas in spring.

Photo, Andrew Besley. By kind permission of the National Trust

Caerhays woodland garden in spring.
Glendurgan house and garden.

Photo, Tymn Lintell. By kind permission of the National Trust.

Glendurgan garden in spring.
Trebah valley garden.

chose as his architect Peter Frederick Robinson, a pupil of Henry Holland who designed Carlton House for the Prince Regent. Horace Walpole praised the 'august simplicity' of Holland's neo-classical style, where surface decoration was cut back to a minimum in order to enhance the beauty and outline of the overall design. It is no surprise to find his pupil Robinson using the Ionic order at Trelissick, for Holland was particularly fond of it and had already given the Duke of York's splendid Dover House in Whitehall a magnificent Ionic portico. In 1827 Robinson published his *Designs for Ornamental Villas*, and design No. 3 is clearly based on Trelissick.

Thomas Daniell implemented his father's plan to lay out carriage roads through the wood and to plant trees along the Fal estuary. It was an ambitious project whose legacy we enjoy today, but it helped to cripple Daniell financially. His legendary wealth ran out in 1832 and he was obliged to flee to France to escape his creditors. It was a long exile, for he died in Boulogne in 1866. His neighbour across the Fal, the Earl of Falmouth, bought Trelissick but sold it twelve years later to a John Davies Gilbert. Gilbert's son added a second storey to the single storey wings that had been part of Robinson's original design.

When Carew Davies Gilbert died in 1913, his executors let Trelissick to Mr L. D. Cunliffe, one of the governors of the Bank of England; in 1920 he bought the house and part of the estate. He and a French architect, M. Joubert, planned the present solarium. His step-daughter Mrs Ida Copeland inherited the property in 1937 and she and her husband Ronald (whose family firm was W. T. Copeland & Sons Ltd, manufacturers of Spode China) moved from Staffordshire to Trelissick in 1948. The house is now occupied by their son, and **Trelissick gardens** have been given to the National Trust.

Standing at the head of a vast and very beautiful and natural harbour and facing Falmouth across the water, the site of Trelissick is spectacular. The parkland that stretches down to the water's edge was largely planted in the 1820s, although the Gilbert family continued the process. Like the picturesque buildings in a harbour scene by Claude, the graceful silhouettes of the mature oak, beech, and pine trees frame the vista down to the water and gently lead the eye to the middle distance and beyond to the misty waters of the Carrick Roads and the town of Falmouth.

The Copelands were largely responsible for the wonderful gardens to be seen today. Ronald Copeland was a rhododendron expert and planted many of the more tender varieties such as the white and pale pink hybrids raised from Himalayan and Chinese species and *R. griffithianum* or those from *R. cinnabarinum* with their distinctive blue-green foliage. The claret-coloured 'Royal Flush', pink 'Lady Rosebery' and apricot 'Lady Chamberlain' are among the loveliest of the latter category. He also planted a large number of the existing camellias and the very mild climate made it possible to grow tender South American shrubs. Most eye-catching are the creamy flowers of *Drimys winteri*, the crimson *Tricuspidaria lanceolata*, and *Abutilon vitafolium*, a climber with lilac blue flowers. *Halesia carolina*, better known as the snowdrop tree, imported into Britain for the first time in 1756 and named after Dr Stephen Hales, a plant physiologist, has white, 'pearl-drop' flowers, which hang in rows beneath the branches and look like air-borne snowdrops waving in the breeze.

CAERHAYS CASTLE overlooks the cliffs of Porthluney Cove, a small bay between Nare Head and Dodman Point. Both castle and site are supremely romantic. The history of Caerhays is full of romance, too, its early owners having been given to chivalrous deeds and fits of passion.

The Trevanions came to Caerhays in the mid fourteenth century when one of their number married Joan Arundell. The property remained in the Trevanion family through direct descent or through marriage until the end of the seventeenth century when it was pulled down*.

In 1808 John Trevanion asked the architect John Nash to build a vast romantic castle below the old house with pleasure gardens leading down to the cliffs. Such a project gave both men a chance to indulge their most extravagant fantasies. Today, when a thick mist blows in from the sea and presses round the castellated walls, Caerhays looks like a fairy-tale castle floating in the vaporous air. Towers and turrets, round and square, rise up out of the gloom, their ghostly forms silhouetted against dark, dripping trees.

The interior of the castle with its round drawing-room, double staircase and long gallery, was as grandiose in conception as the exterior. The garden plan was equally extravagant. Formal parterres and terraced walks were laid out within the castle walls, while outside paths led through the woods and deer park to an ornamental lake lying between the castle and the sea. Each scheme was more extravagant than the last and, inevitably, Trevanion's resources ran out. By 1824 much of the estate land as well as the house itself was mortgaged to raise money for the building costs. Trevanion was too much in debt for this to be a solution and he left for Brussels, presumably to escape his creditors. He died there in 1840.

In 1853 the unfinished castle, mortgaged to the hilt, was put up for sale and bought by another rich mining family, the Williams of Scorrier. Lands which had for so long sustained the Trevanions were sold off in lots. The final irony was that much of it proved to be fabulously rich in china clay. The Williams family restored the castle (the original contents were lost in a terrible fire) and remain in possession of it to this day.

The Williamses not only preserved Caerhays but made a significant contribution to English gardening. John Charles Williams came to live at Caerhays in about 1886. 'J.C.', as he was called, was one of the first gardeners to realise the exciting possibilities open to him when plant collectors began bringing back shrubs from China and Asia. The garden is based on the plant importations

Trelissick Gardens. Looking southwards to the river Fal

Caerhays Castle, Gorran. Designed by John Nash in 1808 for John Trevanion. 19th-century engraving showing the deer park between the castle and the sea.

made by E. H. Wilson between 1900 and 1910 and by George Forrest between 1912 and 1925, the latter sending much seed direct to Caerhays. Some of the loveliest species of rhododendrons include the pale pink *R. oredoxa fargesii*, the rose-purple *R. davidsonianum* and the fragrant white or shell-pink *R. decorum*, all brought back by E. H. Wilson. There are also wonderful stands of the highly scented tender *maddenii* group, varying in colour from white to pink with or without a yellow blotch, as well as the large-leaved *R. sinogrande* and *R. fortunei*. J.C. raised many successful hybrids at Caerhays, only a handful of which have been named, among them the apricot *R. Royal Flush*, the shell pink *Veryan Bay* and the scarlet *Humming Bird*.

J.C. also experimented with camellias, and crossed Forrest's *Camellia saluenensis* with the *Camellia japonica* introduced to England in the mid eighteenth century. This produced the first of a new race of camellias, the *x. williamsii* group, which are hardier and more vigorous in a cool climate. They include the soft single pink 'J.C. Williams', the deep single pink 'St Ewe' and the double purplish pink 'Caerhays'. Another lovely hybrid is *Cornish Snow*, (*C. cuspidata x C saluenensis*).

Magnolias from China also flourish in the grounds and look like great water-lily trees. *M. mollicomata* and *M. soulangiana* 'Nigra' were crossed to form 'Caerhays Surprise'; the gentle pink *sprengeri* 'Diva' and *sargentiana* 'Robusta' are the parents of the salmon pink 'Caerhays Belle'. There is also a wide range of evergreen and deciduous azaleas from India, Formosa, Japan and the United States of America. Today the introduction of new hybrid camellias from America and New Zealand and the planting of new trees indicate a continuation of the planting tradition.

Shelter belts composed mainly of Monterey pines were destroyed in the gale of January 25th, 1990, causing extensive damage, but thanks to grants from English Heritage and the determination of the owners themselves, Caerhays today looks as magnificent as ever. Carpeted with primroses and celandines in March and April and with pink campion in May, this Cornish woodland seems a wholly natural homeland for a plant collection of unsurpassed richness.

8.
Kerrier

St Mawes lieth lower and better to annoy shipping, but Pendennis standeth higher and stronger to defend itself.

Richard Carew, *The Survey of Cornwall*, 1602

KERRIER'S coastline stretches from Falmouth in the east round the Lizard Point and westward to Prussia Cove and the boundary of Penwith. **Pendennis Castle**, high on a promontory overlooking Falmouth Bay, guards this large domain. In the 1530s, when Henry VIII ordered the castle to be built, the headland belonged to the Killigrew family. John Killigrew was appointed first governor of Pendennis in 1544 and was knighted that same year. Today, Pendennis is considerably larger than its counterpart castle of St Mawes across the water, but they were much the same size originally. Pendennis consisted of a circular keep which housed the garrison, and a domestic block at the back where the governor lived. It was surrounded by a dry moat which was crossed by a drawbridge.

As with all Henry VIII's castles, it fell to the governor to maintain and equip the garrison at his own expense. The Killigrews were negligent in their duties in this respect. In early January 1582 a Spanish ship driven by foul weather into Falmouth haven was obliged to remain there for several days. The temptation was great. Killigrew's men boarded her, stripped her of goods and carried her out to sea. Bolts of holland cloth and leather chairs suddenly appeared in the Killigrews' home. The full facts of this murky affair never emerged, perhaps because John Killigrew, as governor of Pendennis, led the official inquiry.

Elizabeth I built the bastioned outer defences of Pendennis in the late sixteenth century. These included walls round the headland with embrasures for cannon and a stone-faced ditch in front. Intended to keep out the Spaniards whom Elizabeth so feared, these extra defences proved vital at the end of the Civil War, when Pendennis was besieged for five months by the Parliamentarians. In the end it was starvation which forced Sir John Arundell to surrender, not any weakening of the castle's defences.

THE Killigrews remained in control of Pendennis for well over a century, living at **Arwenack**, a house right on the waterfront overlooking the great natural harbour at the entrance to the river Fal. The first governor of Pendennis owned lands that stretched from the river Fal to the Helford Passage and with the tithes of various parishes brought him a handsome income. In keeping with his status as governor, he pulled down the old house and built a new one in its place.

The new Arwenack was not finished until 1567. John died as the last stones were being laid. Built on three sides round a quadrangle, the fourth side was open to the harbour. A castellated gate tower flanked by low walls protected this vulnerable fourth side from attack by sea. Palisades and earthworks surrounded the three landward sides. At the north corner of the house stood another tower pierced with loopholes for bows and muskets; since the house lay at sea-level, Killigrew was taking no risks. A great banqueting hall filled the central section of the house. Here, feasts were held for captains of the many ships that dropped anchor in Falmouth haven, Walter Raleigh among them.*

At the end of the Civil War Arwenack was burned to the ground by its owners in order to prevent the Parliamentarians from using the house during the siege of Pendennis. This selfless act of patriotism did not pass unnoticed, for in 1661 William Killigrew was made a baronet. Arwenack was never wholly rebuilt after the Restoration although it was partially restored to suit the needs of occasional residence, and today it is possible to see part of the Elizabethan shell. Adjacent to it is a new house which has now been converted into a number of flats. Every effort has been made to recreate the appearance of old Arwenack, including a courtyard with little parterres surrounded by neatly clipped box hedges. It is easy to imagine the Killigrews watching the ships unload their cargoes on the wharf. After the establishment of Falmouth as a station for the Post Office packet boats at the end of the seventeenth century, all manner of merchandise was seen on the quayside — gold, wine, and fruit from Spain and Portugal, rum and sugar from the West Indies.

When Sir Peter died in 1704 the Killigrew baronetcy became extinct, his only son having been killed in a scuffle at a Penryn inn. The Arwenack estates passed to his eldest daughter Frances and a century later became the property of Lord Wodehouse when he married Sir Peter's great-great granddaughter Sophia.

TWO other mansions in Kerrier, Carclew and Roscrow, must be mentioned here. The Manor of **Carclew**, which runs down to Devoran creek, belonged to the Daungers family in the twelfth century, but the name died out in the early fifteenth century when the last two daughters married a Renaudin and a Bonython respectively, and became co-heiresses of the estate. The Renaudin line soon petered out, leaving the Bonythons in sole possession of Carclew until 1697 when the last male heir, Richard, died.

Richard Bonython's only daughter Jane married a Penryn merchant called Samuel Kemp, who immediately set about reorganising his wife's considerable assets. He sold off much of her land and started to build a handsome new house with the proceeds. He was never to enjoy the grand home he envisaged for he died in 1728 before the house was completed. Jane, less attached to visions of grandeur, promptly stopped all work upon it. On her death some ten years later she left Carclew to her kinsman James Bonython of Grampound and in 1749 James sold the property to the mining magnate William Lemon.

Pendennis Castle, Falmouth. Built in the 1530s to strengthen Henry VIII's coastal defences.

Princes House, Truro. Designed by Thomas Edwards in 1737 for William Lemon.

Lemon was born of humble family in the tiny village of Breage, near Helston, and became the manager of a tin-smelting house at Chyandour, Penzance. He married well, and in 1724 used his wife's dowry to open a tin mine on land belonging to Lord Godolphin at Ludgvan. It became known as Wheal Fortune and was reputed to have earned Lemon £10,000. Thereafter he moved to Truro and began to work the rich Gwennap copper mines. Impressed by the elegant **Princes House** Thomas Edwards designed for him in 1737 in the centre of Truro, he now engaged this talented architect to alter and complete the half-finished house on his newly acquired country estate.

An engraving of Carclew in Borlase's *Natural History of Cornwall* (1758) shows Edwards' design for the house. A two-storeyed rectangular block set on a basement storey to give it extra stature, it is flanked on either side by a low colonnade. Edwards' use of a grand Ionic portico and small pavilions gives Carclew a decidedly Palladian air. The design of the central block resembles that of Wanstead House in Essex (begun in 1713) by Colen Campbell, an engraving of which Edwards could have seen in Campbell's *Vitruvius Britannicus*, published in 1715. Wanstead was praised by devotees of the Palladian movement for its classical order and simplicity, for its clear cut horizontal and vertical divisions and for its magnificent hexastyle portico, 'the first yet practised in this manner in the Kingdom'. The severity of its design was softened by an elegant balustrade adorned with sculpture along the roofline and by contrasting curved and triangular pediments over the windows in the manner of Inigo Jones. Carclew had none of these refinements and was unduly harsh in appearance as a result.

William Lemon died in 1760, leaving his descendants money, a baronetcy, and a zest for public life. They lived at Carclew for a hundred years, until the name became extinct in 1864 on the death of Sir Charles Lemon. His nephew Arthur Tremayne inherited the estate and continued to improve it. Unhappily, Carclew was burned to the ground in 1934 and only fragments of the façade now remain. Photographs taken before the fire show that the house rivalled Trewithen and Antony in magnificence. The simplicity of the exterior belied the lavish decoration of the rooms inside. A graceful colonnade of Ionic columns — by now the hallmark of an Edwards interior — made the entrance hall as coolly elegant as a Roman atrium. Both hall and staircase were richly decorated with elaborate plasterwork and a further screen of Corinthian columns on the upstairs landing complemented the colonnade in the hall. The theme was one of classical grandeur, but grandeur tempered by the delicate, flowing curves of a wrought-iron balustrade, making a perfect blend of rococo charm and classical austerity.

Magnificent broad-leaved trees and massive rhododendrons still flourish in **Carclew Gardens**. In addition visitors can see effective new plantings of golden yew, red maple and berberis.

A FEW dilapidated outbuildings are also all that are left of **Roscrow**, a mile inland

Carclew, near Mylor. Altered and completed by Thomas Edwards *c*. 1750 for William Lemon.Engraving from Borlase's *Natural History of Cornwall* (1758).

from Penryn, although a modern house has been built in its place. Those readers familiar with the writings of Mary Delany, the famous eighteenth-century diarist who laid bare her soul in her *Autobiography and Correspondence* published a hundred years later, will remember that it was to old Roscrow that she was taken in 1718, as the young bride of Alexander Pendarves, a gouty sixty-year-old to whom she was unhappily married.*

This is how she described the old house:

The castle is guarded with high walls that entirely hide it from your view. When the gate of the court was opened and we walked in, the front of the castle terrified me. It is built of ugly, coarse stone, old and mossy, and propt with two great stone buttresses, and so it had been for threescore years. I was led into an old hall that had scarce any light belonging to it; and on the left hand of which was a parlour, the floor of which was rotten in places, and part of the ceiling broken down, and the windows were placed so high that my head did not come near the bottom of them.

It would seem that Roscrow had changed little since Tudor times, and still kept its semi-fortified appearance. However, Mary was allowed to fit the house up to her own liking, and for a time the task of modernising and redecorating took her mind off her situation, but she found it hard to be cheerful. The high grey walls of Roscrow made it a prison, separating her from her family and from sanity.

Only when her beloved brother and mother came to stay or when her husband was away could she see Cornwall in a kinder light. Relieved of Alexander's presence, she became aware of the countryside and, despite its associations, admitted that Roscrow was a beautiful spot:

It was placed on the side of a hill [which fell gently from the front of the house] surrounded by pleasant meadows, which by an easy descent opened a view to one of the finest harbours in England, generally filled with shipping. The prospect was enriched with two towns [Penryn and Flushing] one considerably large and a castle [Pendennis] placed on an eminence which at some distance looked like an island. The chief town [Penryn] was a peninsula, and situated on a high hill; it consisted of one large street which crossed the summit of the hill, by which advantage every house had a falling garden and orchard that belonged to it; and what is yet more singular, a rivulet that ran through each. These gardens and orchards entirely covered the hill, so that to every eye which beheld it at a distance the whole appeared a garden, and in great bloom at its proper season. Indeed nothing could be more delightful or beautiful in the month of May or June; the whole terminated in an unlimited view of the sea.

But a view, however beautiful, was not enough to sustain her, and after her husband's death in 1724 Mary never set foot in Cornwall again.*

BETWEEN Carclew and Roscrow lies another great estate. **Enys**, a Celtic word for an island (it lies at the base of a peninsula between Mylor and Penryn creeks), still belongs to the Enys family who took their name from the place in the eleventh century. An engraving in Borlase's *Natural History of Cornwall* shows a large E-shaped Elizabethan mansion with projecting wings standing on flat ground. A long, formal garden with two pavilions at the end – one survives as a garden cottage – leads to woodland on one side, while cattle graze in the distance. Samuel Enys, Sheriff of Cornwall in 1709, married the daughter of a rich London merchant. When her two brothers died without heirs, Dorothy inherited a fortune. She and Samuel enlarged the house and laid out the gardens. These were famous in the eighteenth century when Borlase made his engraving.

The present house was built in the 1830s upon the old foundations. Henry Harrison, who worked at Port Eliot, was the architect, but the new Enys house was a commission of a different kind. He built a handsome square block whose simple but satisfying proportions are the perfect counterpoint to the flamboyant garden that surrounds it. Parts of the old house – an oak-panelled room, staircase, and windows – still survive at the rear, but otherwise Enys is Victorian loftiness and solidity at its best.

Winding paths overhung by magnolias and rhododendrons as well as rare specimen trees surround the house on three sides, affording colourful views from all the main reception rooms. The long drive is flanked for half a mile by a jungle of deep crimson rhododendrons which rise to over forty feet. On the other side, Pendennis promontory can be glimpsed in the distance. Far below the house, at the bottom of a deep dell that is smothered in bluebells in May, are a series of rectangular ponds fed by a stream. Wild duck live in this gigantic water-garden, and primulas, water-lilies, and yellow iris grow on its banks.

Enys, near Mylor. Engraving from Borlase's *Natural History of Cornwall* (1758) showing the E-shaped Elizabethan mansion.

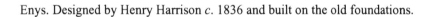

Enys. Designed by Henry Harrison *c.* 1836 and built on the old foundations.

HOUSES and gardens of a different kind, more intimate and informal, are to be found on either side of the Helford River, that slender tongue of tidal water that flows from the mouth of the sea to the little village of Gweek with its two bridges that span the high tide mark. Ancient manors and farmsteads alike were usually built at the steep head of a hidden valley, where level ground might be found. Their gardens sloping down to the edge of a creek are often outstandingly beautiful.

Glendurgan, on the north side of the river across the water from the village of Helford, is one such magic place. The existing house belongs, as it always has done, to the Fox family. Built in the 1840s after the original small thatched cottage had burned down, its owner, Alfred Fox, planted the garden in the 1820s and '30s and designed both the curved drive and walled garden, now filled with roses and fruit trees.

As the chief shipping agents in Falmouth, the Fox family had every opportunity to ask travellers to bring back exotic trees from all parts of the globe. One of the most beautiful introductions is a large *Michelia doltsopa* from Tibet, its multi-petalled white flowers opening in April. Other trees from China include the *Davidia involucrata* and many magnolias. Tender and even sub-tropical plants grow happily in the open in this sheltered climate, and shrubs quickly become trees.

Certain conifers flourish particularly well in a warm, damp climate, and Glendurgan has many of them. Alfred's fifth son, George Henry Fox, planted the Deodar and Atlas cedars, the swamp and Mexican cypresses and the weeping spruce, some of whose trunks have twisted into fantastic shapes. Two tulip trees, *Liriodendron tulipifera*, compete with the conifer for sheer size, their trunks of thickly knotted bark as fat as the sturdiest oak or beech.

Half-way down the garden, in a dip between the steep slopes of the valley, a maze of laurel confuses and delights. Below this is a pond. In early spring arum lilies flower on one side, while on the other the gigantic leaves of *Gunnera manicata* from Brazil spread over the water like huge fans later in the summer. Japanese maples and rhododendrons line the path from the maze to the pond.

GEORGE Henry's cousin Robert Fox of nearby **Penjerrick** raised many hybrid rhododendrons (the original grove of *R. barclayi*, named after his son Robert Barclay Fox, still survives in this equally lovely garden, now open to the public), which found a home at Glendurgan. The fragrant creamy yellow 'Penjerrick' by the pond is one of the loveliest. On succeeding to the property in 1931, Cuthbert Lloyd Fox planted Asiatic rhododendrons, magnolias, camellias, hydrangeas, and eucryphias in a series of glades down the valley slopes. Brilliant flashes of red and orange catch the eye, glinting like the panes of a stained-glass window. Particularly arresting are groups of the purple-blue flowered Chinese species rhododendron *R. augustinii*, and the orange-yellow *azalea luteum* seen against a

Glendurgan garden, sloping down to the Helford river.

backdrop of magnolias and white cherry trees from Japan.

A gate leads to the hamlet of Durgan, a handful of cottages on the quayside and the first point on the Helford River where landing is possible whatever the state of the tide. A steep, leafy lane leads from Durgan along the eastern slope of Glendurgan, and half way up another gate brings you back into the garden.

IN the 1850s Charles Fox created another great garden in a steep ravine just west of Glendurgan. **Trebah**, as it is called, did not remain in the Fox family for long and as a consequence suffered from years of neglect due to changes of ownership. This situation changed in 1980 when Major and Mrs Hibbert bought both house and gardens. Realising before long the tremendous potential of the valley, they decided to spend their retirement magnificently restoring and replanting the gardens and securing their future by establishing the Trebah Garden Trust. Today, the view from the terrace is a tribute to their endeavours and will to succeed.

The visitor begins his descent through an extensive water-garden that has been created on either side of the stream that tumbles down to the mouth of the river Helford some two hundred feet below. Huge tree ferns and phormiums from New Zealand form an exotic backdrop to drifts of white arum lilies and yellow candelabra primula along the water's edge. Agapanthus, beschornerias, aeoniums and agaves cover steep banks on each side of the dell. These clump-forming perennial succulents normally found in hot dry climates seem to thrive on these rocky slopes.

May is a magical month to visit Trebah. Huge clumps of the fragrant yellow *azalea luteum* scent the air, made headier still by enormous trusses of every kind of rhododendron, many of which overhang the paths. These range from the earlier flowering red species *R. arboreum* to many beautiful hybrids from the Loderi group (one of the loveliest being the soft-pink scented *King George*) or the Penjerrick group, raised at nearby Penjerrick. Further down, paths criss-cross the stream through thickets of different varieties of bamboo — *phyllostachys*, *pseudosasa*, *arundinaria* and *fargesia* types. As one emerges into the sunlight the graceful silhouette of a large Pocket Handkerchief Tree, *Davidia involucrata*, frames the vista ahead, its delicate white bracts a necessary foil to the riotous colours of the surrounding rhododendrons. The last stretch of path runs alongside nearly three acres of blue and white hydrangeas which extend the flowering season until Christmas. Overlooking the small beach is a simple granite monument to the officers and men of the US 29 Infantry Division who embarked from Trebah in June 1944 for the D Day assault on Omaha Beach in Normandy. In pensive mood one begins the steep climb back to the house, grateful that one is free to enjoy this corner of paradise.

Other valley gardens which command fine views of the river Helford are **Carwinion** (near Mawnan Smith) and **Trelean** (near St Martin-in-Meneage). The latter is renowned for its planting of cornus, acers and other shrubs for autumn colour.

TRELOWARREN, the home of the Vyvyan family for over five hundred years, is set in gently rolling parkland to the south of the Helford River. The manor was held by the powerful Cardinans in the thirteenth century but passed by marriage to the Ferrers family in 1279. The Ferrers remained at Trelowarren until 1426, when Honor Ferrers married John Vyvyan, whose family came from the parish of St Buryan in Penwith. Indictments for assault, murder, and wrecking show the early Vyvyans to have been a wild and lawless lot, but John's inheritance of Trelowarren brought them respectability and a place in Cornish society. His son Richard married Florence Arundell of Trerice, and in 1544 his grandson Michael was appointed Captain of St Mawes Castle, which was then nearing completion.

Michael Vyvyan died in 1561 and was succeeded by his second son John, who brought vast new estates to the family upon his marriage to a co-heiress of Edward Courtenay, Earl of Devon. He and his bride began to rebuild the mediæval mansion and the walls of the three bays of the chapel that now adjoins the house, including the outer door with its pointed arch and naively carved spandrels and lintel, are all that remain of the earlier building. Some years later, in 1636, Richard Vyvyan secured a licence to restore the chapel and arranged to enlarge the house still further. Work was interrupted by the Civil War in which John Vyvyan's descendant Richard played a prominent part. Charles I commissioned him to coin money (coin being made from plate contributed by

Royalist supporters) and he set up mints at Truro and Exeter. He was also in command of a fort erected on Dennis Head to guard the Helford River. Its construction was financed largely by Richard himself, who gave over £9,000 of his own money to the Royalist cause. Already knighted after a court masque in 1636, Charles I conferred a baronetcy upon him at Boconnoc in 1644. His wife became Lady-in-Waiting to Queen Henrietta Maria.

Sir Richard completed his proposed enlargement of Trelowarren after the Restoration, which he commemorated by setting up two stone pillars in the quadrangle formed by the chapel and the north wing, the old Tudor portion. These pillars now form the entrance gate. He also built a two-storey bay on the garden side, the date 1662 being clearly inscribed beneath the parapet. At some stage an extra bay was added to the east or entrance front, and the large north wing was built in the nineteenth century. Sir Vyell Vyvyan, the 7th Baronet, was responsible for the interior decoration of the old chapel in the Gothic style at the end of the eighteenth century. The interior of Trelowarren is largely Victorian.

Sir Vyell was also responsible for planting the original grounds, but the gardens at Trelowarren are largely the creation of Clara Vyvyan, the second wife of the 10th baronet, Sir Courtenay Vyvyan. Clara had a deep feeling for nature and a passionate love of her home which she conveys in her many books about Cornwall. In *The Old Place* she describes her struggle to keep up the garden after her husband's death in 1941 and following a period of total neglect during the war when Trelowarren was requisitioned. She returned from Bristol to find 'tents pitched, trenches dug, pipe-lines laid all anyhow, nohow' in the midst of 'our wild garden that we call the Pleasure Grounds'. A cess-pit had been sunk in her prize snowdrop patch, and valuable shrubs which had taken her years to establish were either decimated or lost in the undergrowth.

Dismayed but not defeated, Clara and her gardener George, who believed that 'plants and trees is living things and can feel the same as we do', slowly untangled the shrubs and stripped the ivy from the trees. Gradually the Pleasure Grounds — a long, narrow strip of flat ground running from east to west above the garden front — were restored to order, and the paths through the glades cleared. They were tended lovingly until Clara's death in 1976 but are now semi-overgrown once more. The 1662 wing and the chapel are leased to an ecumenical charity called the Trelowarren Fellowship which is responsible for the maintenance of the house, but sadly the upkeep of more than a mile of pathways is beyond its means.

Clara's spirit lives on in the Lady's Garden, a square enclosure to the northwest of the house and bounded on the south 'by a little iron fence separating it from lawn and chapel'. Essentially a summer garden, Clara filled its five flowerbeds, four triangular ones at each corner and one circular one in the middle, with old garden favourites: lilac, yellow aconites, pink tree-peonies, gladioli, roses and wood anemones grew side by side, while round the walls were

Trelowarren, to the south of the Helford river. Engraving from Borlase's *Natural History of Cornwall* (1758) showing the east (entrance) front and the two-storey bay (dated 1662).

Trelowarren. The west front, with the enclosed Lady's Garden on the left and the chapel on the right.

scented plants such as sweet verbena, rosemary, and broom. The plants were of little botanical value but to Clara they were close friends.

A FEW miles inland from Mount's Bay, as the long curve of Kerrier's western shore is called, between Marazion and Helston, stands **Godolphin House**, one of the most historic buildings in Cornwall.

Godolphin is hidden among the trees on the lower slopes of Godolphin Hill, where the tin which made the family's fortune was mined. 'No greater Tynne works in all Cornwall than be on Sir William Godolcan's ground', was Leland's comment when he visited Great Work Mine in 1536. Sir William's nephew, Sir Francis Godolphin, who inherited the estate in 1575, brought in two mining experts from Germany to supervise the sinking of shafts and to explain new techniques. The introduction of processes such as wet stamping and blowing meant that the tin was mined more economically and more efficiently.

The existing fabric of the house was largely built by Sir William Godolphin in the 1530s. Godolphin is marked as a fortified house on Henry VIII's *Great Map of the West* of 1538. It was constructed around two main courtyards, the smaller of which still survives. A study of the four sides of the little quadrangle reveals the alterations made over the centuries. The east side is Tudor, to judge by its round-headed windows, and contains the original dining-room. Its superb linen-fold panelling and carved beams and bosses are finely wrought, and between the windows hangs the royal coat of arms of Henry VIII, said to have been presented to Sir William Godolphin for his services at the siege of Boulogne in 1544. The battlemented wall of the south side represents the original main elevation of the house. An archway in this wall has late Gothic panelling on the jambs and once led to a screens passage and the great hall, enlarged in the late Elizabethan era at a time when the family was growing in status. Sir Francis was Governor of the Isles of Scilly and was responsible for rebuilding an artillery fort known as Star Castle on St Mary's in 1593. At Godolphin, to the west of the forecourt, he built a handsome stable block which has survived, together with the remains of the deer course or Slips, a two-furlong rundown from the deer park on the hill, flanked by a raised terrace walk from which to watch the coursing and by the system of walls which enabled the hounds to pursue and catch the deer.

The elaborately carved fireplace in the early seventeenth century King's Room on the west side of the courtyard was made to commemorate the marriage of Sir Francis's son, Sir William Godolphin to Thomasina Sidney (originally the Great Chamber, this handsome room was converted into a royal apartment soon after 1600). The colonnade of the north front was the last part to be added and was built in about 1635 by William and Thomasina's son Francis. Eight massive Tuscan columns on the outside and six on the inside of the courtyard form an imposing double loggia over the Elizabethan wall and entrance gateway with its

Godolphin House, between Marazion and Helston. The east and south sides of the inner courtyard, showing the round-headed windows of the original Tudor dining-room and the Gothic archway that once led to an Elizabethan great hall.

Godolphin House. The west side of the courtyard, with early 17th-century mullioned windows. On the right, the colonnade of the north front, built *c.* 1635.

Godolphin House. Engraving from Borlase's *Natural History of Cornwall* (1758) showing the colonnaded north front, forecourt and Elizabethan stables to the west.

heavy oak doors. These granite pillars carried a whole range of entertaining rooms with fine views over the forecourt. Stairs at either end indicate the probability of twin sets of apartments with a shared saloon between them. Today the arrangement of the partitions is late Georgian.*

In 1766 the Godolphin estates passed by marriage to the Osbornes, Dukes of Leeds, and gradually declined. In 1804 a large part of the house, including the sixteenth-century great hall, was pulled down. Empty for long periods throughout the nineteenth century, Godolphin was finally sold in 1921. Bought in 1937 by Mr Sidney Schofield and his wife Mary, it has been cherished ever since.

THE land surrounding **Pengersick Castle**, on the outskirts of modern-day Praa Sands, bordered that of the Godolphins. In the fourteenth century Henry de Pengersick, known as 'Le Fort', married Engrina Godolphin. Records testify to his strength and fiery disposition; he was excommunicated from the church for attacking the vicar of Breage and a monk from Hayles Abbey, when they came to collect their dues. On his death in 1343 Pengersick passed to his daughter Alice, and again, through the female line, to the Worth family and then the Milliton family from Devon.

Towards the end of the fifteenth century Pengersick was rebuilt as a fortified Tudor manor, the remains of which still stand today. The letter W worked into the moulding round the uppermost window in the tower suggests that the construction took place in Thomas Worth's time. A drawing made by William

Borlase shows the original design of this building viewed from the main courtyard. Because it was situated so close to the sea and in a low-lying position, Pengersick was vulnerable to attack from marauding buccaneers. The design of the tower, with its four square rooms one above the other reflects the need to have some defence. A 'drop-slot' was inserted over the entrance doorway so that boiling oil or molten lead could be poured on the unwelcome intruder, and access to the entire house was through one small first floor door. This doorway now connects the tower with the modern wing adjacent to it. A broad newel stair leads up to roof level, and a small battlemented turret — a convenient place to store weapons in time of crisis — covers the door onto the leads. From the roof the occupants could survey the countryside from all sides and warn the household of the enemy's approach. The gun room, just below the ground floor level of the tower, is fitted with six arched embrasures which have unusual dumb-bell shaped gun-loops. The enemy had little chance of ascending the tower and gaining access to the rest of the house.*

The first John Milliton's grandson William married Sir William Godolphin's daughter Honor. She arranged for the panelling of the main room to include a series of verses carved in the wood. Both panelling and verses have long since disappeared (although fragments were found in nearby outbuildings), but Borlase made a copy of the verses which has been preserved.

> When marriage was maid for vertew and love
> There was no devorse goddis knote to remove
> But now is muche people fallen into such luste
> That they do break Goddis wyll most juste
> Wherefore unto alsuch let thys be sufficient
> To keipe God is lawe for feare of his punishment
> In the burning lake where is most of all torment.

Tragedy befell Pengersick when William and Honor lost their only son at sea. When William died in 1571 the property was left to their six surviving daughters. As often happens when an estate is divided into impractical units or when daughters have husbands with properties of their own the inherited property is neglected. Pengersick Castle quickly fell into disuse. In time the fortified tower decayed and the materials were used to build cottages nearby. Mouldings from one of the castle doorways can be seen round the front door of the adjacent farmhouse.

By the time the Duke of Leeds's properties came on the market in 1922, Pengersick had become part of the Godolphin estate. The castle was little more than a hollow shell throttled with ivy and used as shelter for cattle. The purchaser restored the tower and built a small modern wing beside it. An effort was made to recapture the atmosphere of a Tudor garden. Trees were planted

Pengersick Castle, Praa Sands.
A reconstruction of the original plan,
drawn by William Borlase.

Pengersick Castle. The late 15th-
century fortified tower.

destined for topiary work, and a series of rising terraces led to a reconstruction of the original arched entrance to the outer court as seen in Borlase's drawing. The present owners completed the restoration work and cherish both Tudor tower and garden.

NO picture of Kerrier would be complete without reference to a smaller, more modest type of manor house, such as **Truthall** which stands high on a hill plateau behind Helston. In the Middle Ages it belonged to the Nance family, and the original low, rectangular hall-house, now part of the farm buildings, can still be seen. A cross passage runs from front to back with the hall, open to the roof, on one side and a smaller service room on the other with an upper chamber or solar above. The arch-braced collar beam roof and the decorative windows of the hall, with their cusped heads and saddle bars, are remarkably ornate for such a simple house and were surely designed to impress. The entrance doorway, too, is imposing with its heavy roll-moulding round the arch and framing hoodmould. The coarse rubblestone wall and rear doorway of roughly hewn moorstone at the back of the house, in contrast, show no such refinement and make no concession to beauty.

In the middle of the seventeenth century a more up-to-date house was built at right angles to the mediæval dwelling, which was demoted to provide further domestic quarters. The date 1642 is inscribed over the front door, which now has a flat head instead of an arch. The ground floor consisted of two rooms, the front hall and another room behind, while upstairs was a fine parlour with mullioned windows and a fireplace. A handsome nineteenth-century house with light, spacious rooms and wonderful views was built beside the seventeenth-century addition.

Truthall. The 17th-century wing
built at right angles to the rear wall
of the mediæval hall-house
(on the right).

Truthall, near Helston. A window
of the mediæval hall-house.

9.
Penwith

Majestic Michael rises; he, whose brow
Is crowned with castles and whose rocky sides
Are clad with dusky ivy; he whose base,
Beat by the storm of ages, stands unmoved
Amidst the wreck of things — the change of time.

Sir Humphry Davy

ST MICHAEL'S MOUNT, standing proudly on a rocky island in Mount's Bay, changes its mood like magic according to the time of day, the time of year. On a stormy winter's day, when the wind howls and whips up the waves to a white foam, the Mount is a forbidding fortress which has withstood three sieges and stands ready, still, to defend Penwith. Yet on a warm summer's evening the island is bathed in a pink glow, a vision of welcome to pilgrims who have travelled from far and wide to worship at the shrine of St Michael.

In the last Bronze Age Penwith was the most highly populated part of Cornwall and St Michael's Mount an important port and trading centre. Ireland, rich in gold and copper, needed Cornish tin to make bronze axe heads, cooking and storage vessels. Rather than risk a voyage round Land's End, feared for its rough seas and treacherous currents, Irish traders landed their cargoes in the Hayle estuary on the north coast and proceeded overland across gentle hills to St Michael's Mount on the south coast. Natives provided horses to transport the wares and acted as guides over the rough tracks, following the route of the present-day A30 road from Hayle to Penzance.*

Domesday Book contains some evidence that there was a religious community on the Mount in Saxon times, but the earliest record of a monastic settlement dates from 1135 when Bernard Le Bec, Abbot of Mont St Michel in Normandy, built a Benedictine priory high up on the rocky island crag. The foundation was made possible by the grant of lands in Cornwall by Robert, Count of Mortain, William the Conqueror's half-brother, to Mont St Michel. Throughout the Middle Ages pilgrims came to the shrine of St Michael to make a vow or as part of a penance required of them by their confessors.**

In 1275 an earthquake destroyed the original priory church. It was rebuilt in the late fourteenth century and is still used for public worship. Although extensively restored in the nineteenth century, the simplicity of the interior faithfully reflects the austere existence of the monks. The stone tracery of the two beautiful rose windows is original, but the stained glass is Victorian.

When Henry V went to war in France the priory was seized by the Crown as an alien religious house, and in 1424 it became part of an endowment for the Brigittine Abbey of Syon at Twickenham. Thus ended any connection with Mont St Michel.*

After the Dissolution of the Monasteries in 1536, the Mount was leased by the Crown to successive members of the local gentry who acted as governors and were required to maintain a garrison. Its subsequent history was chequered, until its Royalist owners sold it in 1659 to Colonel John St Aubyn, whose descendants live there today. In 1954 the 3rd Lord St Levan handed the Mount over to the National Trust. It is now the home of his son, the 4th Lord St Levan.**

Today tourists flock across the causeway at low tide or pile into small boats at high tide to visit a romantic, fairy-tale home. Despite the addition of a Victorian wing below the original buildings, the external appearance of the castle and chapel has hardly changed since the St Aubyns took possession. The library is in the oldest part of the castle, its two small sash windows ingeniously fitted into the lower portions of the twelfth-century lancet windows. It is easy to imagine the monks staring through the narrow slits out to sea, offering silent prayers perhaps for a brief respite from the merciless wind. The Chevy Chase room is named after the seventeenth-century plaster frieze depicting hunting scenes based on the mediæval *Ballad of Chevy Chase*. The hounds sniff furiously and rabbits cock one ear or emerge timidly from their burrows. The room was originally the monk's refectory, the chairs being nineteenth-century copies of those used by the monks. Shields bearing the coat of arms of prominent Cornish families hang on the walls, for the St Aubyns were linked by marriage to the Bassets, Grenvilles, and Arundells. The first St Aubyn owner of the Mount, Colonel John St Aubyn, married the second daughter of Sir Francis Godolphin of Treveneague, and over the castle entrance are the arms of the St Aubyn family impaling Godolphin.

The ruined Lady Chapel was converted into the present Blue Drawing-room between 1740 and 1750 by the 3rd baronet, a Member of Parliament with a reputation for incorruptibility. Incorruptible may be, but compulsively in tune with the fashions of the time, he created an elegant interior in the latest fanciful 'Gothick' style with 'Gothick' Chippendale chairs to match — all in pastel blue and white. Cornish gentry may have been aware of Horace Walpole's Strawberry Hill, a fashionable dilettante haunt being decorated at the same time, but few would have had the chance to visit it. No doubt local families longed to be invited to some entertainment at the Mount in order to inspect and pronounce an opinion on the new style — so light and frivolous compared to their own dark-panelled drawing-rooms.

The 3rd baronet was also a practical man determined to help the local inhabitants. In 1727 he rebuilt the Mount harbour in order to stimulate the export of Cornish tin and copper. A hundred years later fifty-three houses had been built and a thriving fishing industry established. Most of these cottages were pulled down in the early twentieth-century and replaced by the two rows of cottages standing today. A small herd of cows was kept on the island in Victorian times, the milk made into butter and clotted cream in the octagonal dairy, which the visitor passes on the way up to the castle. Stores and fuel are still taken up by means of an underground railway built at the turn of the century.

On the north, more protected and landward side of the island a natural rock garden surrounds the steep path up to the castle. Sturdy pines, evergreen oaks and sycamores manage miraculously to with-stand the wind and give shelter to mature camellias, azaleas and rhododendrons. These shrubs owe their existence to the trees, for without a buffer they would be flattened or uprooted by the relentless wind. New shelter belts are desperately needed to secure the future of the garden in years to come, but considerable thought goes into the buying and positioning of new trees. The Japanese *Pinus Thunbergii* has shown itself to be the most wind and salt resistant. The present Lord St Levan hopes to establish a new type of Dutch elm apparently immune to the dread disease.

Some of the terraces on the eastern side of the island were laid out two hundred years ago. Today these tiny terraces which face south contain an astonishing variety of plants. Different types of aloe adorn the precipice below the castle, the lovely orange *aloe arborea* flowering in February. In the summer mesembryanthemums, ivy-leaf geraniums, and blue convolvulus dangle over the rocks and fill every crevice.

The series of miniature walled gardens formed by each level of terraces are full of surprises. As you look down at them from the castle battlements, the sea, not the rock face, is the backdrop to the gardens, its colour changing from midnight blue to peacock according to the colours of the sky. Muted Cezanne greens come next to blues, for the grass grows to the water's edge, a broad swathe being cut to form a path right round the island. The monks are thought to have established the sweet-smelling Mount lilies (a type of narcissus) which cover the grassy lower slopes in spring, to be followed in summer by masses of blue agapanthus and red hot pokers.

Above this semi-wild domain the terraces become more formal, more man-made, as if to deny or defy the power of the sea. Veronicas, shrub roses, marguerites, pelargoniums, and wall flowers struggle to keep their petals behind hedges of escallonia and fuchsia, while higher up, in a middle zone which the wind somehow by-passes as it wages war on the castle above, a number of rare and tender plants bloom relatively unperturbed. Among the most remarkable are the blue passion flower *passiflora caerulea*, *bigonia grandiflora* and *bigonia cupensis*, *stauntonia latifolia*, lion's paw from South Africa *leonotis leonurus*, *sparmannia africana* and *clematis flammula*. Now the planting continues. Lord St Levan, his head gardener Mr Bowden and their adviser from Tresco, Helen Dorrien Smith — a triumvirate as tough and tenacious as the plants — direct proceedings. Their optimism, determination and imagination have protected and embellished the

St Michael's Mount *c*. 1880, before the trees were planted.

St Michael's Mount. The Blue Drawing-room.
Photo, John Bethell. By kind permission of the National Trust.

most unusual garden in Cornwall.

THE truly spectacular gardens at **Trengwainton**, five miles away on the mainland, are an extraordinary contrast to the windswept Mount and show what a gardener's paradise Cornwall can be. Originally belonging to the Arundells of Trerice, the property was bought in 1814 by Sir Rose Price, the son of a wealthy Jamaican sugar planter. Price planted the trees, mainly beech, ash and sycamore which now stand round the house and grow beside the drive to the lodge and entrance to the gardens. This mature wood is a beautiful natural setting for all the shrubs subsequently planted, and provides the shelter so conspicuously absent on St Michael's Mount. It is an exotic and enchanted world.

William Wilberforce's Emancipation Act of 1833, which abolished slavery, ruined the Price family's fortunes, and the estate was sold in 1867 to T.S. Bolitho, a banker with substantial mining interests. His son, Thomas Robins Bolitho, enlarged the hitherto modest house to its present grand proportions in 1897, and built the wide carriage drive. His nephew, Edward Bolitho, inherited Trengwainton in 1925, and had the daunting but exciting task of creating a garden. He sensibly sought the advice of other Cornish gardeners, notably J.C. Williams of Caerhays who gave him rhododendrons and other shrubs. George Johnstone of Trewithen then suggested that Bolitho should take a share in Kingdon Ward's 1927-8 plant-collecting expedition to north-east Assam and the Mishmi Hills in Upper Burma. Many of the huge rhododendrons and magnolias were raised from seed gathered on this expedition.

On the right of the drive are a series of inter-connecting walled gardens remarkable not only for the amazing variety of the shrubs, but also for the sheer size to which they have grown. In February and March the boughs of tall, graceful magnolia trees from Japan, Sikkim, China, and Tibet are laden with pure white, pale pink, rose-coloured, or purple blooms. One by one the huge but fragile petals flutter onto the path or grass below. Sweet-smelling eucalyptus and acacia from Tasmania, *Styrax japonica* from Japan, with its white, bell-shaped flowers, evergreens from South America and the Himalayas, passion flowers, fuchsias, azaleas, camellias and rhododendrons are carefully nurtured within these walls.

Further up the drive is a small meadow planted with trees in honour of the royal family — a fine oak commemorates Queen Victoria's Diamond Jubilee in 1897, a lime tree Edward VII's coronation in 1901. Queen Elizabeth the Queen Mother planted a Bhutan pine with long bluish-green needles in 1962 and Princess Anne a Mexican pine in 1972, both large trees now.

Magnificent rhododendrons — white, scarlet, deep crimson, magenta pink and yellow — flank the drive and lawns round the house, rivalling beech and sycamore in height. Beyond the lawn in front of the house is a view of St Michael's Mount framed by dark pink and vermilion rhododendrons. This extensive, open vista gives Trengwainton an airy, informal elegance. Situated in a part of Cornwall known for its moors and stony hills, where only furze and bracken grow, this ninety-acre garden is a luscious oasis of rich reds and pinks and shiny, succulent greens.

At the turn of the century a stream garden was created along the edge of the woodland and parallel to the drive. The high humidity and warmth of the Cornish climate provide ideal conditions for the moisture-loving candelabra primulas, king cups, yellow and white skunk cabbage and rodgersias which thrive in large drifts by the water's edge. Different kinds of euphorbia, crocosmia, astilbe and hemerocallis look magnificent against the luscious evergreen backdrop of tree ferns such as *Dicksonia antarctica* and the finer-leaved *Woodwardia radicans* that flourish beneath the canopy of trees. The stream garden is rewarding to visit in spring and later summer when blue and white hydrangeas extend the flowering season.

ROSCADGHILL near Newlyn, the largest fishing town in Cornwall in the nineteenth century and famed for its school of artists, is a fine, late seventeenth-century house with a neat, symmetrical façade. A Cornish (granite) version of a redbrick William and Mary house complete with small, circular lawn and gravel sweep in front, the whole is enclosed by its own wall. The pedimented front door and well-proportioned sash windows on either side show a sound understanding of the new classical concepts of architecture based on symmetry and proportion. The wealthy gentry were the first to respond to the new ideas, but by the late seventeenth century the movement had begun to influence the design of modest houses, and the circulation of pattern books enabled country builders to work in the new style. The sash windows at Roscadghill are not yet flat-headed but are delicately rounded at the top, a reminder of curves and arches soon to disappear altogether.

NEARBY, on gently sloping ground above Newlyn, stands **Trereife**, a house of handsome proportions rebuilt by John Nicholls, a successful Middle Temple barrister, in the early eighteenth century. Having seen the fine Queen Anne houses being built in London with regular brick or stone faces, Nicholls understandably wanted the main elevation of his own home to be as elegant as granite would permit. He thus took the trouble to face the east front with squared rough-cut brown granite and he used the same brown granite for the arches over the window openings elsewhere. The sliding sash window was at the height of fashion and therefore used for the east front whereas casement windows with heavy wooden mullions were used for the west and north sides of the block. Nicholls also raised the first floor of the earlier house to make the two storeys of equal height and put in a new roof with dormer windows. The result is a classical composition of seven bays, the central bay enhanced by a pedimented

Trengwainton garden.
The drive.

Roscadghill, Penzance.
A Cornish granite
version of a William
and Mary house.

porch with Doric columns.

The desire for symmetry is also reflected in the original lay-out of the garden. Contemporary engravings in the dining-room show ladies and gentlemen strolling along straight paths which formed two neat rectangles in front of the house. These are flanked by avenues of trees. The clipped yew hedge that virtually hides the south front was planted in 1780.

Today the garden is softer in appearance. A flat lawn in front of the house leads the eye to the fields beyond where horses graze contentedly. On one side, on a raised terrace, a wide herbaceous border runs the length of the original walled kitchen garden, now used as a paddock. At the bottom of the bank is an equally long border devoted to old-fashioned roses. On the other side of the lawn is a woodland shrubbery filled with mature camellias and rhododendrons.

The Nicholls family continued to live at Trereife until the end of the eighteenth century. In 1799 the widow of William Nicholls married the Revd Charles Valentine Le Grice, the eldest son of a Norfolk clergyman. 'CV', as he was affectionately known by the family, was educated at Christ's Hospital, London and Trinity College, Cambridge. Urbane, witty and intellectual, he thrived in the company of his school friends Samuel Taylor Coleridge, Charles Lamb and Leigh Hunt. Those who knew him assumed he would pursue a literary career. Shortly after taking his degree, however, Charles Lamb noted that 'Le Grice went to Cornwall, cutting Miss Hunt [Leigh Hunt's sister] completely'. Was it to remove himself from an awkward situation or merely the pressing need to earn his living that caused CV to accept a post as a tutor to the son of the widowed Mrs Nicholls of Trereife?

Whatever the circumstances surrounding his arrival, CV proved to be the ideal successor to the Nicholls family. He ran the estate efficiently and played an active part in local affairs, both as a magistrate and as a curate. He died in 1858, having outlived his wife and stepson by more than thirty years. His only son, Day Perry, inherited the estate. His great-great grandson Timothy Le Grice lives at Trereife today.

FARMERS, like the gentry, were not immune to the pressures of fashion. **Trenow**, high on the slopes above the picturesque village of Gulval, is a simple farmhouse of thatch and cob rebuilt in the eighteenth century with all the latest architectural features — at least on the outside. The façade is symmetrical, the roof hipped, and the windows have the new sash frames. But the central front door opens, not as at Roscadghill, into an entrance hall with elegant reception rooms on each side, but into a large kitchen. A small parlour leads off to the right, while the whole of the other side was in fact a cow house with a barn above, reached by stone steps at the back. The façade was not allowed to interfere with practical needs and disguised the real nature of the building.

CORNISH farmsteads and cottages present a mixture of styles and are difficult to date. The sites of these sometimes lonely dwellings whether, moorland hollow or sheltered valley, were probably selected at the beginning of the Christian era when early Celts began to leave their hilltop strongholds to settle further down the slope and to cultivate the land. These early farmers reared cattle, sheep, goats, and pigs, heaving the granite boulders from the land and building stone walls around the tiny fields they tilled.

The Celts continued to live in their humble homes even after the Saxons had replaced the Celtic form of clan ownership with their own feudal system. Today, driving over the bleak hills towards Zennor and the sea, you pass scattered, dilapidated-looking farm settlements — Bosulval, Carnaquidden, Kerrowe — dating from Celtic times. The windy, narrow roads, once rough tracks linking homestead to homestead, sometimes bisect the farm whose buildings are huddled together on each side. Some of the farmhouses were rebuilt or altered in the seventeenth or eighteenth century when the owners prospered, but the barns and outbuildings have a mediæval air. Cob — a mixture of clay, chopped straw, and even slate rubble which bound together the rough, smallish stones that a man could lift himself — was a cheap and far less durable alternative to granite and few early examples of peasant farmhouses have therefore survived, although the walls of a mediæval house will often have been incorporated into a later farmhouse. The thirteenth or fourteenth century long-houses of turf, stone, and wattle remain part of Lanyon farm, near Morvah, where a low partition separates the byre from the main room. The front entrance was shared by man, woman, sheep and cow.

The engine-houses of deserted tin mines are the only companion of these lonely farmsteads. Standing desolately on the rugged cliff's edge or high on the moor, they punctuate the barren landscape from St Just to St Agnes, their tall chimney stacks, like Tuscan campanile, silhouetted against sky and sea. Tin-streaming was flourishing again in the first half of the fourteenth century, bronze church bells and cannons, among other things, being in high demand. New trade routes had opened up, not only through the Cinque Ports to Marseilles, but via Bruges to Venice, Constantinople, and the Near East. Cornish seamen shipped the tin in small boats which hugged the coast to London, where it was transferred into French or Italian ships for the channel crossing. In 1305 mining areas were divided into tracts of unenclosed land known as stannaries and a coinage town allotted to each. The area round St Agnes was part of the Tywarnhayle stannary, while Kerrier and far-flung Penwith combined to form another stannary, with Helston as its coinage town. Twice a year, files of packhorses laden with blocks of tin would plod slowly over the criss-cross moorland tracks towards Helston, where merchants, tradesmen, and pewterers assembled to watch the royal officers weighing and stamping the tin.

In early times, the lord of the manor merely received a toll from any tinner

Trebah. *Gunnera manicata.*

St Michael's Mount. One of the terraced gardens.

Trereife.

Trengwainton. The stream garden.

Tresco Abbey Gardens. A terraced walk.
Tresco Abbey. The pebble garden.

Trenow, Gulval. A Georgian farmhouse of thatch and cob.

or blower who wanted to work on his land. Profit or loss was the tinner's affair. Few of these mediæval lords, although they boasted coats of arms, had houses of any real size or grandeur. The remains of a house belonging to the Godrevy family in Gwithian, north of Hayle, shows how humble the homes of the minor gentry were. Excavations show a dwelling hardly more than a single long room about thirty feet long by twelve feet wide divided by a wooden screen, one side allocated to the family, the other to the livestock. In about 1400 this hovel was modernised and given a stone wall instead of a screen. The sheep and cows were banished to a separate barn and their shed converted into another room with a solar above, reached by a ladder from the hall. This simple abode was the manor house of **Crane Godrevy**. Early in the sixteenth century sand began to pile up and blow into huge mounds and the house was abandoned.

THE eighteenth century was a different story. Some landowners became fabulously rich when tin or copper was discovered on their estates. Two of the largest mines, Cook's Kitchen and Dolcoath, were controlled by the Basset family. A profit of £7,040 was said to have been made in one exceptional month, providing ample funds to build a grand country house on the site of their hitherto modest seat at **Tehidy**, near Redruth. Thomas Edwards, the architect so popular with the Truro mining magnates, was engaged in 1734 to design the new building.

   An eighteenth-century engraving of Tehidy shows a huge, square Georgian

Gulval, c. 1870. A thatched cottage.

Gulval, c. 1870. Rubblestone cottages.

mansion with a pedimented central block and four detached angle pavilions, each with a cupola and clock. No expense was spared. Quantities of brick as well as cargoes of Portland stone, yellow Bath stone and even Purbeck squares were brought by sea to Hayle and transported to Tehidy in two-wheeled wagons. A park was landscaped and the stream flowing along the valley to the sea at Godrevy was fed into an excavated area to the south of the mansion to form a lake. Cascades were built in the river outlet and boats were provided for the family and guests. Grandiose in conception, Tehidy was a suitably elegant residence for a family whose lineage went back to Reginald de Dunstanville, Earl of Cornwall in the twelfth century.

John Pendarves Basset did not live to see his new house completed. He died of smallpox in 1739, aged twenty-five, leaving his widow Ann with £100,000 from mineral profits and rents. His brother Francis inherited Tehidy and his son Francis was created Lord de Dunstanville in 1796. A handsome portrait of him by Gainsborough hangs in the blue drawing-room at St Michael's Mount. Dressed in a ruffled shirt and mustard yellow waistcoat, he looks a cultured, sensitive man whom one can imagine entertaining in style.

Lord de Dunstanville died in 1835 with no male heir, and the estates passed to a nephew. The mansion remained unchanged until 1863 when John Francis Basset, whose dues from his various mines were yielding £20,000 a year, decided to enlarge it. Italian artists were commissioned to paint and gild the ceilings of the new drawing-room, dining-room and billiards room, while new servants' quarters were added in the basement beneath. For a few short years life was carefree and glamorous. Then fate dealt a series of blows from which the Bassets never recovered. Mental illness had dogged the family ever since the marriage of Francis Basset to Margaret St Aubyn in 1756. John Francis Basset died in 1869, his brother Arthur committed suicide as his father had done in 1870 and his brother Walter was declared insane. One remaining brother, Gustavus, produced an heir, Arthur who celebrated his coming of age in 1894 with a magnificent ball held in the large pavilion erected for the occasion. Its walls were covered with cream-coloured fabric over which were draped curtains and swags of terra cotta, electric blue, crimson and gold materials hung between large mirrors. This dazzling event was to be the last of its kind at Tehidy.

High taxation, a reduced income from a depressed mining industry and Arthur's unbridled passion for horse-racing and betting made it increasingly difficult to maintain Tehidy and the shortage of ground staff during the Great War precipitated the downfall of this once great estate. Arthur moved to Henley Manor in Crewkerne and the following year, in November 1916, the estate was divided into separate lots and sold. The house became a hospital for the treatment of tuberculosis in 1919. A month after the first five patients had been admitted a terrible fire virtually destroyed the mansion. Only the square angle pavilions of Thomas Edwards's house survive, together with a number of outbuildings. The

Tehidy, near Redruth. Engraving from Borlase's *Natural History of Cornwall* (1758) showing the elegant mansion designed by Thomas Edwards c. 1750 for the Basset family.

Tehidy. 19th-century engraving of the garden front.

modern porticoed building dates from 1919. Only the long, wide approach to the house conveys the property's former splendour.

MORE modest houses are to be found in the lush green valleys between Penzance and Land's End. For centuries farmers worked the small arable and grass fields which go right down to the cliff's edge and are protected by stone hedges now covered with great clumps of yellow gorse and a myriad of wild flowers. With the advent of the railway in the mid-nineteenth century, many of these fields were turned into market gardens which supplied not only vegetables but flowers for the cities 'up-country'. In springtime these fields were ablaze with every kind of daffodil, blue and red anemones, and violets, each valley transformed into a huge and glorious garden. Today, because transport and labour costs have soared, it is no longer economical to pick and sell flowers. The daffodils have to compete with the steadily encroaching bracken and brambles which threaten to smother them completely. For the moment, however, delicate white, sweet-smelling narcissus and golden double daffodils are left to bloom in semi-wild state, and when viewed from afar become a stunning patchwork quilt of every shape and shade of white, yellow and orange.

Trewoofe farm in the valley of Lamorna was once surrounded by such fields and orchards. In the sixteenth century Joanne de Trewoofe and her husband Thomas Lavelis enlarged the house into an E-shaped Elizabethan manor, with a richly sculptured central doorway surmounted by the arms of both families to commemorate their marriage. Their heirs lived at Trewoofe until the end of the seventeenth century when the last male heir was drowned while up at Oxford. By 1706 the manor and its lands had been split into three parts and sold to local families. The west wing was pulled down and rebuilt in the old herb garden; the east wing, though altered in the eighteenth century, still stands. The central portion, with its magnificent doorway, suffered because insufficient land went with it to make it economically viable. It was sold in a derelict state early this century, but its present owner's love and care ensure its preservation.

PART of a fifteenth-century manor house belonging to the Keigwin family still stands in Mousehole. Its deep porch of rather crudely fashioned granite columns surmounted by an upper storey dominates the tiny cobbled street. In 1595 four Spanish ships suddenly appeared off the coast and landed 200 men who razed Mousehole to the ground. Only **Keigwin Manor** survived the onslaught, being built of stone and not cob. Jenkin Keigwin fought to the death to defend it.

THE village of Mousehole, a tangle of narrow, twisting streets which climb steeply upwards from the sea, boasts a proper harbour wall and small wharf. **Penberth Cove**, a smaller fishing community, is tiny in comparison and completely different in atmosphere. Most of the cottages in the wooded valley

Mousehole c. 1880. Children playing outside a 15th-century manor house that belonged to the Keigwin family.

and on the cliff go back to the seventeenth century and one is still thatched. No modern houses spoil the old-world feeling, for the National Trust ensures that no new building takes place. The cove itself is a natural harbour. Steeply rising cliffs on either side shelter the inlet, and the boats are hauled safely to the top of a tiny slipway where the fish is weighed and packed.

From the eighteenth and nineteenth centuries huge shoals of pilchards arrived off the shores of Penwith in August and September. Huers, whose task it was to sight the shoals, shouted directions in front of their cliff-top hut to the men in their boats below. The pilchards were netted in long, cumbersome seine nets and dragged ashore to be salted and packed. The men heaved the fish out of the boats with wooden shovels and carted them in barrows to the pilchard cellars, which can still be seen to the left and right of the slipway. They resemble a row of cottages from the outside but, in fact, the ground floor of each is a cellar. When the doors are open, you can see the floors of black elvan stone on to which the pilchards were tipped. Elvan is even harder than granite and much finer in texture. Large slabs were brought by boat from the Lizard and slotted in rows, end-up like tombstones, to make a deep, non-porous, long-lasting floor. Stacks of pilchards, each layer carefully salted, remained in the cellar for five or six weeks oozing oil (used for cooking and lighting lamps), which trickled along wooden gulleys in the floor and down into wooden barrels.

Women came from as far afield as St Just to press and pack the pilchards for export in barrels to Italy and other Mediterranean countries. All pilchard profits went to the squire or parson who had set up the company and supplied the boat and nets. The huers and seinesmen who did the work and braved the weather were merely paid for their services. Few were fishermen; they were mostly farmhands or miners taking time off.

. In the early 1900s the pilchard shoals disappeared and never returned. Penberth men turned to lobster and mackerel fishing and grew daffodils, anemones and violets in the valley in order to make ends meet. The sons of the fishermen learned a trade to safeguard against hard times. Today, when unemployment in trade is high, they return to fishing. Whereas twenty years ago there were only three full-time boats, now there are eleven. The fish is sold by individual boat but the men have devised a co-operative system of fishing. They need each other to push the boats into the water and so the boats always go out and return together. They rely on the 'Captain' to work the electric winch which pulls the boats back up the slipway and they take it in turns to drive the lorry, bought collectively like the winch, into Newlyn where the catch is sold.

EARLY this century the lane leading down to the cove consisted of rough, granite stones worn into position by carts trundling up and down the valley. This tiny road still follows the swiftly flowing brown-bedded stream that tumbles into the sea by the slipway. Half-way down to the cove, the stream is bridged by a solid-looking gatehouse. This is the entrance to **Penberth**, an early twentieth century house built in a long, low semi-circle facing the sea.

The drive sweeps up to the house in a graceful arabesque, past a natural rock garden crammed with dwarf azaleas, rhododendrons and hydrangeas, the stream forming a natural boundary between the garden and the road. Designed to enjoy the presence of the sea yet to suggest a retreat from it, it is from the verandah that the setting of this exquisite garden is best appreciated. The lawn below slopes gradually down to the cove, narrowing finally to a grassy path beside which are the ruins of an old mill-house. Called Melynon, meaning the mill in the valley, it is mentioned in King Athelstan's charter, dated 943, to the monks of St Buryan. Shrubs of every kind flank the little paths round the lawn but camellias take pride of place. There are some forty species at Penberth, the dark crimson *C. japonica altheaiflora* being one of the most beautiful.

ANYONE who has read Daphne du Maurier's *Rebecca* will remember Manderley, the great house to which Maxim brought his shy young second wife. They motored down from London in early May, 'arriving', as Maxim said, 'with the first swallows and bluebells' and turned into the drive which threaded like a ribbon before them.

Penberth Cove c. 1880. The pilchard cellars.

Penberth Cove today.

Above our heads was a great colonnade of trees, whose branches nodded and intermingled with one another, making an archway for us, like the roof of a church. Even the midday sun would not penetrate the interlacing of those green leaves, they were too thickly entwined, one with another, and only little flickering patches of warm light would come in intermittent waves to dapple the drive with gold.

I sometimes wonder if Daphne du Maurier might have had **Boskenna** in mind when she wrote *Rebecca*, for the approach to it fits the description so perfectly. Two sturdy granite pillars guard the entrance to the drive, which runs in a straight line deep into the heart of a wood. In winter-time, trees shudder and creak in the wind, their trunks and stunted branches bent pathetically towards the land, as if struggling to escape from the relentless gales. Hundreds of daffodils and primroses line the drive in March, and in May the trees celebrate their survival by forming a canopy of green over a carpet of bluebells. Huge turquoise blue and white hydrangeas flourish in the autumn shade.

The drive bends in the distance and turns again. Round the last corner, trees give way to shrubs and the approach broadens into a gravel sweep with a simple granite sundial in the middle. Solid and rambling, Boskenna is not quite Manderley; its modesty would be out of place in a romantic novel. The square porchway, designed to keep out wind and wet, is unobtrusive, its smoke-grey granite walls starkly bare. The irregular roof-line, proof of later additions to the seventeenth century core, give the house an informal air. It belonged to William Carthew in the sixteenth century and passed to the Paynter family in the seventeenth. Paynters lived here for 200 years until the 1950s when to pay off huge loans, the estate was broken up and the farms sold.

Lawns flanked by large borders, a colourful hotch-potch of flowering shrubs and perennials, lead round to the other side of the house, more uniform in shape with its two gable ends and tall mullioned windows. Outside the library and drawing-room a path runs through the trees to the glistening sea beyond. Garrulous rooks cackle noisily, but do not disturb the peace of Boskenna, which was my childhood home and where my love of Cornwall, its people and traditions, its wildness and poetry, its houses and gardens began.

THE making of **Tresco Abbey Garden** began in 1834 when Augustus Smith took up residence as Lord Proprietor of the Scilly Islands, having leased them from the Duchy of Cornwall. Augustus built his house high above the ruined arches and walls of a Benedictine priory and called it Tresco Abbey. Turning his mind to the garden, he started to carve a series of terraces and steps out of the south-facing hillside, skilfully using the natural outcrops of granite to give added drama to the site. Windbreaks mainly of Monterey pine (*Pinus radiata*) and Monterey cypress (*Cupressus macrocarpa*), as well as hedges of holm oak (*Quercus ilex*) were then planted to the west and north-east to keep the salt-laden winds at bay.

Boskenna. The drive.

Boskenna.
The entrance front.

By the 1890s Augustus had succeeded in establishing a dazzling array of trees, shrubs and perennials from all over the southern hemisphere, courageously growing many of them for the first time out of doors in the British Isles. Despite major catastrophes in 1987, when sub-zero temperatures and freezing winds killed much of the plant material, and in 1990 when the hurricane decimated the shelter belts, the garden today is as beautiful as ever. Heartened by the natural regeneration of many of the species thought lost and excited by the opportunity to plan and plant new areas, Robert Dorrien-Smith and his head gardener have taken the garden forward in a very positive way. Botanic gardens from all over the world, and private gardens too, have given them plant material as rich and diverse as before.

Tresco's poor, sandy soil suits perennial succulents such as aeoniums, agaves, beschornerias, oscularias, kalanchoes and furcraeas, all of which thrive on the rocky terraces. Equally remarkable is the collection of protea, leucospermum and banksia, (evergreen shrubs grown for their colourful flowerheads) which are planted against a background of tree heathers, leucadendrons and eucalyptus. Bromeliads, distinguished by their bold, usually rosetted, and often, spiky foliage, include the greeny-turquoise *Puya alpestris*, the yellow *Puya chilensis* and varieties of dyckia and hechtia.

Tree echiums from the Canary Islands and Madeira send up rocket-like spikes in summer, the most spectacular form being the red *E. wildpretii*, while South Africa is represented by swathes of homerias, watsonias, agapanthus (which have spread naturally in the sand dunes), pelargoniums and different types of the daisy (*compositae*) family such as *gazania*, *felicia*, *arctotis* and *dimorphotheca*.

Metrosideros trees from New Zealand are well suited to this mild, maritime climate, their coppery-scarlet flowers making a wonderful contrast to the greens of the tree ferns and cordylines. The 1987 winter killed all the acacias from Australia and Tasmania but there are now sixty-five different species back in the garden. Particularly lovely is the vivid yellow *Acacia verticillata*, nicknamed 'Prickly Moses' because of its whorled, needle-like phyllodes. Also from Australia are various species of eucalyptus, one of the most eye-catching being *E. ficifolia* which bears deep red flowers in summer. When the garden is seen in bright sunshine, with glimpses of the shining sea from the upper terraces, the risk involved in planting so many tender species is amply justified. Aflame with hot reds, yellows, pinks and crimsons in high summer, the garden affirms not just the richness of the sub-tropics but Cornwall's age-old defiance of the elements.

Bibliography

I am grateful for the use of material from articles by Christopher Hussey, John Cornforth, Mark Girouard and others in *Country Life* and by Michael Trinick in the Royal Institute of Cornwall Journal and a number of National Trust publications.

I have consulted the following books:
Borlase, W. *The Antiquities of Cornwall* 1754, *The Natural History of Cornwall* 1758
Brendon, Piers *Hawker of Morwenstow* Jonathan Cape 1975
Carew, Richard *The Survey of Cornwall* 1602
Chesher, V.M.& F.J. *The Cornishman's House : An Introduction to Traditional Domestic Architecture in Cornwall* D. Bradford Barton, Truro 1968
Clarendon, Edward Hyde, Earl of *The History of the Rebellion and Civil Wars in England* (Ed. W. D. Macray) 1888
Coate, Mary *Cornwall in the Great Civil War* D. Bradford Barton, Truro 1933
Delany, Mary *Autobiography and Correspondence of Mary Granville, Mrs Delany* (ed Rt Hon. Lady Llanover) 1861.
Du Maurier, Daphne *Vanishing Cornwall* Victor Gollancz 1967, *Rebecca*
Evelyn, John *The Life of Mrs Godolphin* Ed. 1847
Fiennes, Celia *The Journeys of Celia Fiennes* (ed. C. Morris) 1947
Fisher, John *The Origins of Garden Plants* Constable 1982
Gilbert, Davies *The Parochial History of Cornwall* 1838
Girouard, Mark *Life in the English Country House: A Social and Architectural History* Yale University Press 1978
Gore, Alan and Fleming, Laurence *The English Garden* Michael Joseph 1979
Grigson, Geoffrey *Freedom of the Parish* Anthony Mott 1982.
Halliday, F.E. *Richard Carew of Antony* Melrose 1953, *A History of Cornwall* Duckworth 1959
Hardy, Emma *Some Recollections* (ed. Evelyn Hardy and Robert Gittings) Oxford University Press 1979
Harrison E. *Gunners, Game and Gardens* Leo Cooper 1978
Hawker, R. S. *Footprints of Former Men* 1870
Henderson, C. *Essays in Cornish History* Clarendon Press, Oxford 1935
Jenkin, A. K. Hamilton *The Cornish Miner* Allen & Unwin 1927
Kingsley, Charles *Westward Ho!* Dent 1976
Journals of the Royal Institution of Cornwall (various)
Lake, W. *Parochial History of Cornwall* Truro 1868
Leland J. *Itinerary* (ed L. T. Smith) 1906
Lysons *Magna Britannica*
Norden, John *Speculi Britanniae: Cornwall* 1728
Pevsner, N. *The Buildings of England:* Cornwall 1951
Polwhele, R. *The History of Cornwall* 1803
Redding, C. *Illustrated Itinerary of the County of Cornwall* 1852
Rowse, A. L. *Sir Richard Grenville* Jonathan Cape 1937, *Tudor England* Jonathan Cape 1941, *The Byrons and Trevanions* Weidenfeld & Nicholson 1978
Tangye, Michael *Tehidy and the Bassets* Truran 1984
Tolstoy, Nicholas *Half Mad Lord, Thomas Pitt 2nd Baron Camelford* Jonathan Cape 1978
Twycross, Edward *Mansions of England and Wales: County of Cornwall* 1846
Vyvyan, J. L. *The Visitations of Cornwall* Exeter: Wm. Pollard & Co 1887
Vyvyan Clara C. *The Old Place* Museum Press 1952, *Helford River* Peter Owen 1963

Appendix

p6*   The *Mary Rose* was the second largest ship in Henry VIII's fleet that assembled at Portsmouth in 1545. When French ships sailed suddenly into view the English fleet, taken by surprise, prepared to attack. As the *Mary Rose* went into action she began to heel over to port. The sea poured into her open lower gunports and she sank immediately. Roger Grenville and her entire crew were drowned.

Now the *Mary Rose* has been brought to the surface and her contents closely examined. Did the pewter wine flagon, the candlesticks and gold coins found in the officers' quarters aft belong to her gallant captain? And did he use the small wooden gaming board and the tiny pocket sundial made of boxwood that have survived more than four hundred years under the sea? These tangible reminders of life on board make Roger's death more poignant.

The age of Elizabeth I seemed to suit the energetic, restless Grenville temperament and test its mettle. It was a time when men could fight or explore the world in the service of their country, a time when heroism and honour had meaning.

Sir Richard Grenville is Kingsley's hero in *Westward Ho!*, where there is a description of him strolling in the garden of old Stowe with his young godson Amyas Leigh, to whom he gives fatherly advice on the dangers and rewards of falling in love:

At one turn they could catch, over the western walls, a glimpse of the blue ocean flecked with passing sails; and at the next, spread far below them, range on range of fertile park, stately avenue, yellow autumn woodland, and purple heather moor. . . A yellow eastern haze hung soft over park, and wood, and more. . . And close at home, upon the terrace before the house, amid romping spaniels and golden-haired children, sat Lady Grenville herself, the beautiful St Leger of Annery, the central jewel of all that glorious place, and looked down at her noble children, and then up at her more noble husband, and round at that broad paradise of the West, till life seemed too full of happiness, and heaven of light.

As sheriff and loyal servant to the Queen, Sir Richard made it his business to expose and arrest Cornish Catholics and to keep a sharp look-out along the coast for boats landing Jesuit priests from Douai or Rome. In the 1570s fierce legislation was introduced to counteract the papal bull of excommunication which ordered all Catholics to withdraw their allegiance to Elizabeth I. It became an act of treason to celebrate mass, and anyone caught doing so was severely punished.Staunch Catholics were driven underground and many were ready to die for their faith. Sir Richard Grenville was feared and hated by these brave men, for he showed them no mercy.

Sir Richard is chiefly remembered as a seafaring man, a friend of Sir Walter Raleigh and rival of Sir Francis Drake. Appointed by the government to supervise the defences of Cornwall upon the outbreak of war with Spain in 1585, Sir Richard was chosen to chase off any Spanish ships found lurking in the Irish Channel after the Armada had been sighted off the English coast in July 1588. It was a hard and dangerous task, for violent storms swept the Irish coast that autumn and twenty of Spain's finest galleons were shipwrecked.

When Drake's expedition to Lisbon failed, Sir Richard seized his chance and in 1595 set off as vice-admiral on the *Revenge* to capture the Spanish *flotas* or treasure fleets which passed through the Azores from the Indies *en route* for Spain. The English ships patrolled the seas for four months waiting for the *flota* to arrive. By then sickness was rife. While they were in the midst of disinfecting the ships with vinegar and bringing clean ballast on board, Spanish ships from the Armada appeared out of the blue and attacked. Raleigh's report indicates that Sir Richard refused to turn tail, which would have been to 'dishonour his self, his country and her Majesty's ship', and faced the enemy bravely. The fighting was heavy, Sir Richard remained on the upper deck until midnight, when he received a severe head wound. By morning the noble *Revenge*'s masts were torn and the powder had virtually run out. Sir Richard was all for sinking the ship with what remained, 'that nearby nothing might remain of victory or glory to the Spaniards', but the Captain and master refused to let him and he was taken aboard the Spanish flagship. He died a day or two afterwards.

p6** Sir Richard's grandson, Sir Bevil Grenville, was equally courageous. He succeeded to Stowe in 1636, a few years before the Civil War, and was the first to raise King Charles's standard in the West and call his tenants to arms. Under Sir Ralph Hopton, he led the Cornish forces to victory at Braddock Down in January 1643, and followed this with another success at Stratton, a few miles to the south of his beloved Stowe. The fact that he knew every hill, wood, and dell so intimately proved invaluable as he orchestrated the battle and rounded up over a thousand prisoners. Two months later this gallant soldier was mortally wounded at Lansdowne near Bath, together with fellow Cornishmen Godolphin and Trevanion. This was the turning point of the Civil War in the West, for with the death of these charismatic leaders the fighting spirit and will of the Cornish soldiers weakened.

John Grenville defended the Scilly Isles until their final surrender to Cromwell in 1651 and then went into exile. He was allowed to return to Stowe in 1659, mistakenly trusted by the Parliamentarians, for he began at once to plot their overthrow. He had appointed a relation of his, Nicholas Monck, as rector of Kilkhampton and immediately sent him to Scotland to persuade his brother, General George Monck, to help restore Charles II to the throne. Monck and Grenville met secretly, exchanging messages from the King, and on 1st May, 1660, Grenville delivered a letter from Charles to both the Commons and the Lords. The Restoration was under way.

p13* Wrecks were a common occurrence on this savage north coast. Between the years 1824 and 1874 as many as eighty vessels were swept on to the rocks round Bude. The *Caledonia*, with a crew of ten, was wrecked off Sharp's Nose, a headland just south of Morwenstow, in 1842. Hawker helped carry the dead up the cliff 'to await, in a room at my vicarage which I allotted them, the inquest', and cared for the sole survivor, Edward Le Dain of Jersey. The figurehead of the *Caledonia* — a white-painted wooden figure brandishing sword and shield — still rests over the captain's grave in Morwenstow churchyard.

The ghosts of drowned sailors whose bodies were laid out in the lychgate house for burial haunted Hawker, and yet he was drawn to the sea. The hut he constructed from the timbers of wrecked ships still stands on the cliff. When the weather was clement he would sit here in his claret-coloured coat, fisherman's jersey, and long sea-boots and meditate on the paradoxes of the world about him. Here too, he would read aloud to his wife and compose his poetry, much of it filled with images of the sea.

p23*   In 1483 Richard Edgcumbe, together with other prominent Westcountrymen, joined the Duke of Buckingham in an attempt to overthrow Richard III who, it was rumoured, had murdered the two sons of Edward IV in the Tower of London. The revolt failed. Savage storms prevented Buckingham from crossing the Severn on his way to Exeter and he was caught and executed without trial at Salisbury. The same storms made it impossible for Henry Tudor to land and he was forced to return to Brittany. All those implicated in the plot were outlawed. Edgcumbe took refuge at Cotehele where he was eventually tracked down by Richard III's dreaded local agent, Sir Henry Bodrugan. Miraculously he managed to slip through the cordon, and fled towards the river by a steep path that is today part of the Cotehele garden. He saved himself by filling his cap with stones and flinging it into the water so that Bodrugan's henchmen, in hot pursuit, thought he had jumped in and drowned. When his pursuers had gone Richard sailed quietly away to Brittany to join his King.

Two years later, Henry Tudor landed at Milford Haven and won his crown at Bosworth Field. Richard Edgcumbe was knighted after the battle and made Comptroller of the Royal Household, Chamberlain of the Exchequer and Member of the Privy Council. At the same time he acquired the estates of Sir Henry Bodrugan near Mevagissey.

p33*   Richard was a man of letters. Virgil, Homer, Pliny, Holinshed, Chaucer, Spenser, Marlowe, and Shakespeare were his companions and he taught himself Greek, Dutch, French, Spanish and Italian. He so enjoyed 'sweet relished phrases' of Italian that he set about translating a long poem by Tasso which was published in 1591.

His fame rests above all on his *Survey of Cornwall* (1602), an account of the topographical, political, social, and economic structure of the county. He is a shrewd observer, witty and outspoken. Crammed with interesting facts, the *Survey* is also full of amusing anecdotes which tell us much about the workings of an Elizabethan gentleman's mind. His duties as justice of the peace, deputy-lieutenant of the militia, and sheriff of Cornwall took him all over the county at a critical time in English history. A Spanish invasion was a constant threat. There was panic at Antony when news came that the 'Spanish floating Babel' to quote Carew, was nearing Plymouth. His friendship with other members of the gentry involved in public service kept Carew up-to-date on all the local gossip and gave him first-hand knowledge of matters otherwise outside his ken. Sir Francis Godolphin, for example, supplied him with the information on mining that he needed for his *Survey*.

p33**   'The fish thus taken are commonly bass, mullet, gilthead, whiting, smelts, fluke, plaice and sole,' says Carew, who, like any keen fisherman, is proud of what he has caught. 'The pond also breedeth crabs, eels, shrimps, and [in the beginning] oysters grew upon boughs of trees which were cast thither to serve as a hover for the fish.' Carew would watch these trapped fish for hours, noting their reactions to the food thrown to them and their different swimming patterns according to the time of year.

He even planned, at one stage, to build 'a little wooden banqueting house on the island in my pond'. In Elizabethen times small banqueting houses, of fanciful architecture to match the exotic food served in them, were often built either in a turret on the roof or in the garden. After the main meal was over, the company would retire to these banqueting houses to be served the void (in mediæval times eaten standing as the tables were 'voided') or dessert of spiced delicacies and sweet wine. Carew's banqueting house was to have had a square ground plan, with a round room downstairs and a round turret containing a square room above. A tiny kitchen, buttery, and storehouse for fishing rods led off these two rooms, as well as space for 'cupboards and boxes, for keeping other necessary utensils towards these fishing feasts.' We do not know why such a delightful project was abandoned.

p37*   John Eliot also raised its status when he was knighted in 1618 and made Vice-Admiral of Devon. Unfortunately for him in the course of his duty he arrested a pirate who, as it turned out, had a friend at Court, and it was Eliot who found himself imprisoned. Disillusioned with such corrupt ways he fervently opposed the unconstitutional religious and financial measures of Charles I. In 1629 he refused to pay the King's forced loan and persisted in defending the liberties of the Constitution. For his moral courage he spent the last years of his life in the Tower and died of consumption in 1632. A few days before his death an unknown artist painted him in a lace-embroidered nightshirt, looking resolute and unrepentant. This poignant portrait hangs in Port Eliot today.

p42*   Mystery surrounds Arthur's birth — some say he was cast from a shining ship and borne on a mighty wave to Merlin's feet one dark and stormy night. One of the more popular legends tells that Uther Pendragon, King of All England, fell in love with Ygerne, the beautiful wife of Gorlois, Duke of Tintagel. Uther invited Gorlois and his wife to his castle in Carlisle and, during a lavish entertainment, told Ygerne of his love for her. The lovely Ygerne rejected the King, and she and Gorlois fled back to Tintagel to prepare for a siege. Because of its inaccessible position, Tintagel could be defended by relatively few men, so Gorlois left Ygerne and went to defend his other castle, Terrabil. Here he was killed in a bloody combat with Uther's army, which then went on to overpower the handful of men at Tintagel. Uther forced the unhappy Ygerne to marry him and a son, Arthur, was born.

The babe was handed over to Merlin secretly in a cave on the left of the postern gate of the castle and brought up in his care. When King Uther was dying, the old wizard summoned all the barons to his bedside so that they could hear the King proclaim Arthur his heir. When the barons still fought for the throne, Merlin persuaded the Archbishop of Canterbury to call all the nobles as Malory says, to 'the grettest chirch of London' where, one by one, each had to try to pull a sword out of a steel anvil set in the middle of a marble slab. On the hilt of the sword was written: 'Who so pulleth out this sword of this stone and this anvil is likewise King, born of all England.' Only Arthur succeeded, and he was duly crowned.

Legend has it that the Round Table of King Arthur is buried beneath a circular barrow not far from the main road between Tintagel and Boscastle. This mound was once the site of Bossiney Castle, used as an outpost for Tintagel Castle and recorded in Domesday Book as being held by Count Robert of Mortain.

Tintagel is also associated with the Tristan legend. The twelfth-century poet Beroul, in his *Roman de Tristan*, one of the earliest known versions of the legend, makes Tintagel the residence of King Mark, uncle of Tristan and husband of Iseut or Isolde. The beginning and end of Beroul's poem have not been preserved, but scholars have reconstructed the missing episodes. In this version Tristan became the lover of King Mark's wife.

Iseut then avoided discovery by lying on many occasions but was finally caught *in flagrante dilecto* and sentenced to death. They escaped, however, and after further adventures were finally united. Wagner's opera *Tristan and Isolde* gives a nobler version of the story, and Matthew Arnold's poem 'Tristram and Iseult' is beautiful and uplifting.

Another poem describes how their bodies were brought back to Cornwall and buried in the church of Tintagel, one on each side of the nave. The story is told of two trees that grew miraculously one from each tomb, their branches meeting in an embrace over the apse. Three times King Mark had the trees cut down, and three times they grew again.

p45*   Bishop Grandisson of Exeter, in his Register for 1357, records how, on December 27th, 1356, a host of armed men 'furiously entered the chancel and with swords and staves cut down William Penfound, clerk', and desecrated the church with human blood. The bishop gives no reason for the crime, so we are left to wonder whether William was murdered for corrupt or immoral practices or whether he was set upon by thugs.

The family fared better in the fifteenth century, though not without some narrow squeaks. Documents in the Public Record Office reveal that in 1460 John Wynard of Plymswood Farm (which still stands) 'broke open two of John Penfound's houses and carried away his goods'. He also tried to kill his neighbour, and 'on the following Sunday went with one hundred men to his house' in an attempt to lynch him. What on earth caused such hatred between the two men?

The following year, in 1461, John Penfound was granted the Office of Weigher of tin and lead in Devon and Cornwall for life. A few years later he was granted 'Office of Keeper of the Parks of the King at Hellesbury [now Michaelstowe] and Lanteglos', with a salary of £4 11s 3d. But in 1476 he appears to have gone to London on some wild extravagant escapade with a John Beaumond and was afterwards outlawed 'for failing to appear in the Court of Common Pleas to answer Nicholas Mille, citizen and tailor of London, touching a debt of £150 8s 7d' — a considerable sum of money.

By the sixteenth century the Penfounds seemed bent, by fair means or foul, on acquiring more land. A petition to the Lord Chancellor in 1533 accuses Thomas, William and Edmund Penfound of having unlawfully seized '300 acres of pasture, 300 acres of land, 100 acres of meadow, 40 acres of wood, and 600 acres of furze and heath in Cornwall'. A similar complaint was lodged in 1544 by Crystofer Coke who maintained that Burracott farm (which still exists at the bottom of the hill) belonged to him by right, but that 'Thomas and Edmund Penfound obtained some of the title deeds, forged others and claim the lands'.

p50*   The Mohuns had lived at Hall and Bodinnick, across the water from Fowey, since Edward III's time, and were a respected Cornish family. Sir John Mohun, son of the 1st baronet, was created a peer in 1628 and became Lord Mohun of Okehampton. The title became extinct on the death of his great-grandson Charles, the 5th and last Lord Mohun. Charles had a quick and vindictive temper. He was twice tried and acquitted of murder but his luck ran out in 1712, when he challenged the Duke of Hamilton to a duel in Hyde Park. The two men disliked each other intensely, owing to a disagreement over money, and were resolved to fight to the death. Jonathan Swift mentions the affair in his *Journals to Stella*. Both men seem to have given a mortal thrust at the same instant and both died in a pool of blood. 'While the Duke was over him,' says Swift, 'Mohun shortened his sword and stabbed him in the shoulder to the heart.'

p53* During the last few months of 1642 the Royalist commander Sir Ralph Hopton had organised an army of volunteers, consisting in the main of tenants and servants of the Cornish gentry. This small band, only 1,500 foot with a few guns, was a formidable force prepared to fight with feudal devotion. By November Hopton felt confident enough to advance on Exeter, but the expedition was a failure due to inadequate provision and insufficient discipline, and his men had to retreat to Bodmin. In January 1643 the Parliamentary forces retaliated and crossed the Tamar, the Scottish Colonel Ruthven at their head. Fortunately for Hopton, Ruthven did not wait for the main body under the Earl of Stamford but advanced from Liskeard and drew up his troops on the downs in front of the tiny church of Braddock, not two miles from Boconnoc woods where Hopton's men were encamped.

The battle was soon over. After prayers had been said the brave Royalists advanced, the foot in the centre, the cavalry on the outside. Sir Bevil Grenville suddenly ordered the foot to charge and they did so with such ferocity that the enemy turned and fled. 'But when resistance was over,' wrote Clarendon, 'the Cornish soldiers were very sparing of shedding blood, having a noble and Christian sense of the lives of their brethren.' This first battle on Cornish soil was a resounding victory for the Royalists, whose losses were slight. Twelve hundred Parliamentarians and five guns had been captured, and Hopton wasted no time in attacking and capturing Saltash four days later.

After more than a year of bitter fighting beyond the Tamar, the Parliamentarians returned to Cornwall at the end of July 1644. Their new leader, the Earl of Essex, grossly underestimated the hostility and hatred of the Cornish peasantry, but when King Charles set up headquarters at Boconnoc Essex realised he was done for. The King's men were joined by Grenville's loyal supporters, who had taken Bodmin and were camped at Lanhydrock, while Hopton's army provided more reinforcement. Essex was virtually encircled, his 10,000 men confined to an area of a few square miles between Lostwithiel and the sea.

His only hope was to occupy Fowey and pray for the arrival of more troops by sea, but he stupidly allowed the King to occupy the east bank of the Fowey River, thereby losing control of Fowey itself. By the end of August, after a month of ransacking the houses in the area for food, Essex's men decided to make a dash for it. On the dark, misty night of August 30, the bedraggled foot made their way through the mud to Fowey. They got as far as Castle Dore, some two miles to the north of the port, where they were attacked by the Royalists the next morning. Essex slipped away and sailed for Plymouth in a fishing boat, leaving Skipton, who had brought up the rear with the artillery, to surrender. The terms were honourable but harsh. The wounded were to be sent by sea from Fowey to Plymouth, while the rest of the army was to march out of Cornwall under guard. The Parliamentarians had to suffer not only the abuse of the Royalist army but also the harsh scorn of the Cornish peasants, who stripped them of their clothing and beat them. Only 1,000 out of the 6,000 men who left Lostwithiel reached the safety of Poole in Dorset, for brutality, starvation and exposure took their toll, while the Parliamentarian horse, riding through the night, evaded the Royalists and escaped to Devon. In time this escape was seriously to undermine Charles's victory.

Meanwhile, King Charles and his supporters, who had been showered with honours for their services, feasted at Boconnoc.

p53**   Thomas Pitt was born at Boconnoc in 1775. Separated from his parents, who spent most of their time in London or abroad, Thomas was left in the care of a tutor. Deprived of playmates and human affection, yet conscious of his privileged position as heir to a great estate, he grew to be emotionally vulnerable yet proud. His father died in 1793, soon after Thomas joined the navy, and his career henceforth was both turbulent and tragic. After his death Boconnoc passed to his sister Anne, who had married William Wyndham, Lord Grenville. He died in 1834, when George Matthew Fortescue inherited it.

p53†   Ever since John Glynn had replaced Thomas Clemens as deputy-steward of the Duchy, he had been a doomed man. Clemens bitterly resented his appointment and was determined to make him pay for it with his life. In January 1469 his henchmen beat up Glynn and his servants while he was holding the court of the manor, tore up the court rolls and held him under duress until he signed a £200 bond agreeing not to prosecute his assailants.

The following year, Clemens and his men raided Morval and stripped it of furniture and possessions. John's wife alleged that they stole feather bedding, pillows, tapestries, cushions, silver plate, and 400 gallons of ale. Not content with this, they drove off 14 oxen, 10 kine, 60 bullocks, 8 horses, 400 sheep, and 10 sows from the surrounding pastures. Although the Glynns issued a writ of appeal of robbery against him, Clemens continued to roam freely and a few months later struck the final, fatal blow. His spies informed him that John intended to go to Tavistock fair. An ambush was planned, and at 4 a.m. they pounced on him at Higher Wringworthy and hacked him to pieces. His grieving widow describes these events in a petition to Parliament complaining of the lawlessness of Cornwall. His murderers 'clove his head in four parties and gave him ten dede wounds in his body; and when he was dede, they cut off one of his legges and one of his armes, and his hede from his body'. They also stole his purse, signets of silver, sword, dagger, and even his cloak. Clemens harboured the assailants until they were implicated and then went into hiding himself, but it is not known whether he was ever caught and hanged.

p54*   The main residence of the Trelawnys had been the manor of Trelawney (from which they took their name) in the parish of Altarnun near Launceston. This passed into other hands when the male line of the elder branch of the family died out in the mid fifteenth century on the death of Richard Trelawny. Richard's younger brother John continued the line and his descendant Sir Jonathan, the first of a long line of baronets, settled at Trelawne early in the seventeenth century.

p54**   Bishop Trelawny took holy orders in 1673 and became Bishop of Bristol in 1685. A staunch Royalist like his father before him, he supported James II during the Monmouth Rebellion and remained loyal to the Stuart cause until the King's catastrophic religious policy brought about an irrevocable rift.

In 1687 James II published his Declaration of Indulgence exempting Catholics and Dissenters from penal statutes and, by the use of his dispensing power, introduced both Dissenters and Catholics into all departments of state. The following year he went further and issued a proclamation to force the clergy to read the detested Declaration from their pulpits. This was the last straw as far as Bishop Trelawny was concerned. He and six other bishops refused, and were immediately imprisoned in the Tower. There was uproar in Cornwall while the trial went on, and public rejoicing in the streets when the seven bishops were acquitted and released. Hawker's poem is thought to refer to this incident.

A few weeks later, invited by Protestant nobles enraged at James's policies, William of Orange landed in England. Trelawny swore an oath of allegiance and was rewarded with the bishopric of Exeter and later that of Winchester. He died in 1721 at his residence in Chelsea but his body was brought back to Cornwall and buried at Pelynt, close to the cherished grey stone house of Trelawne.

p54†   The Trelawnys controlled not only fishing rights but the right to unload sand, which with seaweed supplemented the farmyard manure on Cornish farms. Barges fitted with heavy canvas bags kept open by iron hoops dredged the sand from the sea-bottom off Looe or Talland Bay and then proceeded up-river to deposit their load at Trelawne Moor.

As the demand for fertilizer increased, so lime-kilns appeared on the river bank, limestone quarried outside Plymouth being the nearest supply. Behind the kilns between Shallow Pool and Watergate, the nearest point on the river to Trelawne, traces remain of the deeply rutted tracks made by convoys of packhorses as they trod through the Trelawne woods with as much as four hundred pounds of lime straddled in bags across their saddles.

Revenues from the silver and lead mines higher up the valley, under the hills to the north and south of Herodsfoot, were another source of Trelawny income, although no vast fortune was made as was the case with the tin and copper mines further to the west. Shafts were sunk down to the ore-ground in the 1840s, but miners had searched for scraps of shimmering metal for over a century before and continued to do so after the mines were abandoned at the end of the nineteenth century.

In the seventeenth and early eighteenth century the manufacture of Westcountry serge brought considerable wealth to Devon merchants, and evidence of fulling-mills on the Trelawne estate and elsewhere in the Looe river valley shows that this eastern part of Cornwall shared in the trade. The Pelynt weavers would bring their woollen cloth to the fuller, who lived in a cottage of cob behind Trelawne Mill. The fuller's job was to scour, dry and stretch the cloth on racks and then to full or thump it. He would first of all fold the cloth, rubbing it with soap between the folds, and then place it beneath a heavy wooden bar known as the perch, which would hammer the cloth as the water-wheel turned.

p58*   Carnsew was also keenly interested in mining and welcomed Sir Francis Godolphin as a visitor. Unlike Sir Francis, William had no valuable tin mines on his land, but he dabbled in various mining ventures nonetheless. A London company, providing financial backing to prospect for copper, lead and possibly silver, relied on Carnsew for honest on-the-spot intelligence and advice. They sent down a young and rather self-opinionated German mining engineer named Ulrich Frose to oversee work at the Treworthy mine on the coast near Perranporth. Ulrich stayed at Bokelly over Christmas, but the realisation that there was not enough capital to dig deeper made for a somewhat strained atmosphere. The two men got on each other's nerves and Ulrich was no doubt miserable in the cold and damp winter climate. Carnsew never grew rich through his mining activities, but the excitement they engendered outweighed any disappointment.

p64*   John Molesworth was the Queen's Commissioner for the Duchy of Cornwall and married Catherine, daughter and heiress of John Hender of Botreaux Castle, near Tintagel. His grandson settled in Jamaica and eventually became Governor of the colony. William III made him a baronet in 1688, as a reward for loyalty during the religious persecutions which took place in Jamaica during James II's reign. On his death in 1689 the baronetcy and his Jamaican fortune passed to John's elder brother, Sir John Molesworth of Pencarrow.

p68*   High-spirited Emma and her brother used to go fishing for trout in the stream at the bottom of the garden, 'puss always on a little boulder in the middle of the stream — at intervals putting her paws right into the water'. This might seem a childish pursuit for a girl of twenty, but Emma's parents, over-conscious of their former gentility, kept to themselves in their now impoverished state and only visited two families in the entire neighbourhood. Emma thus played with her brothers and kept the one remaining servant, Anne Chappel, company. Anne 'kept a basket of crockery under a tree and a great kitchen table, and we had pleasant reading and working hours and many meals there'.

Modern-day Bodmin does not intrude, and one can imagine her sister's wedding day, as Emma described it. Kirland would have looked its smartest and gayest as the guests clustered round the entrance porch to wave goodbye to the bride and groom. Emma left with them in the dog-cart, for she was to housekeep for her sister. Helen Catherine had married the rector of St Juliot, a remote village on the wild north coast, near Tintagel, and it was here that Emma met Thomas Hardy, a young architect sent to restore the ruined church. Canny old Anne Chappel had prophesied years before that Emma would marry a writer and Helen a vicar. As she left Kirland destiny was taking Emma one step nearer the fulfilment of her romantic dreams.

p69*   Prior Vyvyan was a powerful figure in his day, although the whole ethos of monastic life was changing and the old order was soon to disappear. Lay officials were by now managing the estates belonging to Bodmin Priory — Nicholas Prideaux was Prior Vyvyan's steward or man of affairs — and they were not slow to turn such a position to their advantage in the years before the Dissolution and afterwards. Prior Vyvyan died in 1533 and was succeeded, after much politicking, by Thomas Mundy, canon of Merton Abbey in Surrey. Although Bodmin was far away from London, it was only a matter of time before Henry VIII's grasping agents arrived to strip the priory bare and deprive him of his wealth and privilege. Mundy acted in the nick of time. At midsummer in 1537, he summoned his brethren because 'he did here that the King's Majesty would take his pleasure upon their house, and, therefore, he thought it good to give unto such as had beene good to the house, some leases or other preferments, to the interest they should be the better to them hereafter'.

Mundy's suggestion was even less altruistic than it appears. Those whom he felt should receive 'leases or other preferments' turned out to be his nephew and niece and Nicholas Prideaux. Like Prideaux, Mundy was a bachelor, and the two men planned to tie the families together to the mutual advantage of both. Mundy granted a ninety-nine-year lease on Rialton to his brother John at £60 per year, a very reduced rent. This was a clever move, because the normal lease for a Crown property was only twenty-one years and Henry VIII soon made longer leases illegal because they deprived the Crown of substantial revenues. John Mundy's son William married Nicholas Prideaux's niece Elizabeth, and her brother William Prideaux married John Mundy's daughter Joan, thus securing the Rialton property to both families.

On her marriage to William Prideaux, Joan Mundy was granted a ninety-nine-year lease of the manor, customs, fisheries and advowson of Padstow at an annual rent of £10 7s 8d. In 1544 the freehold of the manor was sold by the Crown to a Londoner, John Pope, for £1,551, perhaps in lieu of money owed.

Pope sold it immediately to Nicholas Prideaux. The expense of war in the reigns of Henry VIII, Mary, and Elizabeth, and the Crown's constant need of ready cash, made the sale of these erstwhile ecclesiastical estates inevitable. By the end of the century almost all had been sold. It was, after all, a unique opportunity for the gentry to acquire more land and hence to consolidate their power.

p74*   Friends of Emma's, Captain and Mrs Serjeant, were living at St Benet's in the 1870s. 'A chapel was within, large, full of lumber, a fine large hall and grandly wide and windowed principal staircase with a spiral stair, all in good repair and very habitable. Nevertheless it was a dark, gloomy and not very healthy abode. . .' Emma seems to have made the most of the library during her stay, though she remarks that no one read the 'much mildewed' books save her.

One wet day I rubbed them dry and enjoyed a good deal of browsing for some days amongst them. There were sloping lawns, terraced gardens, and a fishpond, but everywhere an old-time sadness prevailed. One's soul was not refreshed out of doors, where we were amongst the bones of the former immured people, though no cemetery could be seen or known.

The atmosphere was rendered even gloomier by the doleful presence of the rector who actually owned the place and who was looked after by the Serjeants. He was an invalid and recluse whom Emma never saw, for he remained shut in his room.

Emma does recall one exciting incident which would have temporarily relieved the gloom. Lanivet was

. . . in the heart of the China Clay works, which made the country walks hideous with yellow mud, Stamping Plant always working, and pools and cisterns of white and of green water, and turned-up arid soil — but my friends were enriched by the finding of clay on the estate whilst I was there. A large bowl was brought to us all to look at one evening and pounded and prodded and handled lovingly and chuckled over; it proved to be of excellent quality, whitest of white and pliable and the agent came and settled it all. It was a valuable asset to their income, but if it had all been *under* the house what would they have done?

p74*   After the Prayer Book Rebellion of 1549 and the swift execution of the rebel leaders (one of whom was Humphry Arundell of Helland, a cousin of the Lanherne branch), most of the Cornish gentry accepted the introduction of the new Protestant Ordinal and adapted themselves to the religion required of them by the monarchy. Not so the Arundells, who continued to worship as devout Catholics despite severe persecution. But it was not only their recusancy that set them apart from the other gentry. The Arundells were socially grander than most other Cornish families and moved in elevated circles outside the county.

The 12th Sir John's brother Thomas, who began his training as a lawyer in the household of Sir Thomas More and Wolsey, had married Queen Catherine Howard's sister and bought Wardour Castle in 1547. The 13th Sir John married the daughter of the Earl of Derby, the widowed Lady Stourton, and succeeded at Lanherne. Their aristocratic connections probably affected their relationship with the more modest landed gentry of the county, who either held them in awe or envied their position.

Lanherne was a haven for all Cornish Catholics as persecution gradually forced them underground or abroad. The Arundells harboured many a seminary priest in their households, Catholics coming from far and wide to celebrate mass in secret at Lanherne. For his continued support of the Catholic faith even Sir John, with all his influence at court, was sent to the Tower in 1584, and was kept in semi-custody until his death at Isleworth, near London. His widow retired with her priest to the Arundell estate at Chideock in Dorset, but it was only a matter of time before spies informed the Queen's servants of her whereabouts. The house was searched in 1594 and evidence found to support the suspicion that daily mass was being said, a punishable offence under the Act of 1571. The faithful chaplain was executed, and Lady Arundell retreated to a convent in Brussels.

p76*   Edmund Tremayne, the builder of Collacombe, acted as a kind of westcountry agent of the Queen and was well known at Court. The 4th Sir John may have met him through his father, who spent his life in royal service, and, being pleased with the excellent work of his own plasterer at Trerice, recommended him to Tremayne. The dates on the overmantels support such a theory: 1572 and 1573 at Trerice and 1574 at Collacombe. He may then have gone to Buckland Abbey, the great house of Sir Richard Grenville, for the overmantel in the hall there bears the date 1576 and is very similar in appearance.

After the death of his first wife Katherine, Sir John married Gertrude Dennys of Holcombe and their son, an ardent royalist, became the 5th Sir John Arundell.

He was born a few years after the completion of the new house and Sir John spent most of his life as an M.P., first for the little borough of Mitchell and then for the County. He was sixty-five when the Civil War broke out, but was such an ardent supporter of the King that he was appointed governor of Pendennis Castle after the death of Sir Nicholas Slanning at the siege of Bristol in 1643. Here he harboured poor Queen Henrietta Maria on her flight to France, and later Prince Charles, who escaped to the Scilly Islands only a few weeks before Fairfax demanded the garrison's surrender. The seventy-year old Sir John despatched his reply immediately. 'I resolve that I will here bury myself before I deliver up this Castle to such as fight against his Majesty, and that nothing you can threaten is formidable to me in respect of the loss of loyalty and conscience.' The brave old man held out for five months despite appalling hardships.

Plague broke out and many of the inmates were reduced to starvation. Finally, he wrote to the Prince saying that he could not allow women and children to die of hunger and agreed to Fairfax's terms.

His second son Richard succeeded to a much impoverished Trerice, for his elder brother had been killed at Plymouth in 1643. His father did not live to see the return of the monarchy but soon after the Restoration Charles II remembered his loyalty and that of his two sons by creating Richard Baron Arundell of Trerice. One hundred years later, on the death of the 4th Baron Arundell in 1768, the estate, like that of Ebbingford, passed to his wife's nephew William Wentworth.

p77*   John Robartes was a Parliamentarian, and for a few momentous months in 1644 Lanhydrock was the headquarters of the Parliamentary forces. The 2nd Lord Robartes fought bravely at Edgehill and Newbury and was promoted Field Marshal under Essex. That August his house was seized and occupied by the Royalists and his estates assigned by the King to Sir Richard Grenville. Robartes himself managed to escape by sea to Plymouth, but his children were detained as prisoners. He regained Lanhydrock under the Common-wealth, devoting much of his time thereafter to developing the estate. But he came to disagree violently with Cromwell's decision to rule the country without Parliament and, after Cromwell's death, he played an important role in securing the return of Charles II, for which he was rewarded at the Restoration.

p84*   Times were uncertain during the mid-sixteenth century; years of bitter warfare between Emperor Charles V and François I of France were interrupted by truces no sooner made than violated. Wolsey's policy of courting first one power, then the other, antagonised both. The King alienated himself further by his attempts to divorce Catherine of Aragon, Charles V's aunt, and by his final breach with Rome. François I had no reason to like him either, for England had mounted expeditions to France and was not to be trusted. When the Emperor Charles V and François I resumed hostilities in 1542, Henry joined in on the side of the former. An English army landed on French soil and conquered Boulogne, a foolish undertaking since it achieved nothing militarily speaking but increased the likelihood of a French attack on England.

p86*   John Treffry is said to have captured the French royal standard at the battle of Crecy in 1346. He was rewarded with a knighthood and the right to quarter arms with the French *fleur de lis*. His descendants continued to advance in royal service. Another John Treffry went into exile with Henry Tudor, landed with him at Milford Haven where he was knighted and fought at the battle of Bosworth in 1485. The family then prospered under Henry VII, during whose reign much of Place was rebuilt. John's brother William who succeeded him at Place became Usher of the King's Chamber, Controller of the coinage of tin and Surveyor of Customs within London.

p86**   Thomas was right to fortify his home. A century later the threat of attack from Spain caused John Treffry to assemble pikes, halberds and other weapons at Place. By 1568 Anglo-Spanish relations were strained to breaking point. When Spain sent the ruthless Duke of Alva to crush the Protestant resistance in the Netherlands, England retaliated. Privateers drove two Spanish ships into Fowey harbour. The gold coins on board were taken to Place to be weighed and counted in full view of the townsfolk before being taken to the Tower of London. This treasure, a huge loan from Genoese bankers to the Spanish king, was on its way north to pay Alva's hungry and discontented troops. The Spanish government promptly placed an embargo on English shipping and England counter-attacked by appropriating any Spanish ship in an English port. The treasure was not returned, and Alva's troops mutinied.

p90*   Tantalisingly, although a complete set of architect's drawings have been preserved, they are unsigned and have no precise dates. Nor were many of the designs followed. Records exist, however, of payments to a Mr Edwards, and it is likely that he was Thomas Edwards of Greenwich and the architect of Trewithen. Very little is known about Edwards, and no record has been found of his having designed houses elsewhere in England. Enough evidence exists, however, to show that he managed to build up a considerable practice in Cornwall, and he will be mentioned in subsequent chapters in connection with other houses. His will indicates that he was a mine and ship owner as well as an architect, and these interests no doubt kept him in Cornwall. His association with the mining magnate William Lemon, for whom he designed Princes House in Princes Street, Truro in 1737 and Carclew in 1749, would have led not only to further architectural commissions but to exciting commercial ventures. One can also surmise that Edwards was an admirer or follower of James Gibbs, since he was one of the subscribers to Gibb's *Book of Architecture* (1728).

p92*   Christopher Hawkins started the great East Wheal Rose lead and silver mine near Newlyn East, one of the richest in the county, and established a reputation as a notorious borough-mongerer. He was sole owner of the pocket boroughs of Tregony, Grampound, and Mitchell, obtaining the latter for Sir Arthur Wellesley, later the Duke of Wellington, in 1806. One of the houses in Mitchell is called Wellesley House to this day.
    Sir Kit, as he was known, was a forward-thinking squire who had his tenants' interests much at heart. An early educator in terms of agricultural practice, he laid the first clay-pipe land drains in Cornwall. The patron of Richard Trevithick, he also commissioned the first steam threshing machine for Trewithen. This is now in the Science Museum in London.

p96*   By the seventeenth century the gentry of Cornwall were no longer content merely to receive a toll from tinners wanting to work on their land. They were ready to gamble, and formed their own companies, sometimes owning all the shares so that they could win or lose all. As technology improved the shafts could be sunk ever deeper. Rich lodes of copper were discovered beneath the tin, and in the early nineteenth century, when new high pressure engines, smaller and cheaper, were introduced, there was a spectacular increase in production. Cornwall soon became the largest copper-producing area in the world. The population of Cornwall soared as thousands came to find employment in the tin mines, but working conditions were appalling.

p100*   In 1485 Henry VII rewarded William Trevanion for his Lancastrian sympathies by making him Esquire to the Body of the King. Henceforth the Trevanions were in royal service. William's son Hugh was one of the commissioners appointed to survey Cornwall's coastal defences in 1539, and was also responsible for collecting funds to pay for war and for arresting pirates. Caerhays' coastal position allowed him to keep an eye on activities at sea between Fowey and Falmouth.

Hugh's descendant Jack Trevanion raised his own volunteer regiment at the outset of the Civil War, as did other leading Cornish families. These plucky infantrymen fought every action from Braddock Down to the siege of Bristol in July 1643, when many were killed. The Cornish foot attacked in three brigades — Sir Nicholas Slanning and Trevanion in the centre, Colonel Buck on the right and Sir Thomas Basset on the left. The charge was a fatal one. Buck was decapitated by a halberd, Basset was hit and Slanning and Trevanion were both shot in the thigh with musket bullets and fell immediately. Jack's bravery was remembered by the King when he knighted his father at Boconnoc the following summer, but nothing could make up for the loss of those gallant Cornishmen who perished at Bristol.

One of Jack's sons, Richard, supported James II in the same selfless way, escorting him to France when his luck had run out. Richard supported his unfortunate monarch when he led an abortive expedition to Ireland in 1690, attending him until his death in 1701.

In the eighteenth century the Byron family enters the Trevanion annals. John Trevanion and the 4th Lord Byron married the two daughters of Lord Berkeley of Stratton, Barbara and Frances respectively. John and Barbara's son William was the last male Trevanion. William's sister Sophia married her cousin, the younger brother of the 5th Lord Byron. This marriage, which took place in the chapel adjoining the gatehouse (now demolished) in 1748, marked the beginning of a series of ill-fated relationships. On William's death in 1767 the estate passed to his other sister Frances and her husband John Bettesworth.

Sophia's son Jack, a handsome rake, was the poet Byron's father, and her daughter Fanny's son was later to marry the poet's half-sister Augusta. Then, two generations later a descendant of John and Frances Bettesworth, Henry, married Augusta's daughter Georgiana. Incestuous passion and depravity were the corollary to these disastrous unions which undoubtedly weakened the Trevanions' moral fibre. But Henry's father, John Bettesworth (he assumed the name of Trevanion in 1801), set the final seal on the family's demise when he decided to pull down the ancient seat of Caerhays, which stood to the north of the present castle. This was an emotional and physical blow from which the Trevanions never recovered.

p104* At the time of the Stuarts, Killigrews had considerable influence at court. Sir William Killigrew, eldest son of Sir Robert Killigrew, was a Gentleman Usher to Charles I and commanded one of the two troops of horse which guarded the King during the Civil War. After the Restoration he became Vice-Chamberlain to the Queen and a prolific dramatist. His brother, Thomas, also a dramatist, began his royal service as Page of Honour to Charles I. He was Charles II's Resident in Venice during the Commonwealth years and then in 1660 became Groom of the Bedchamber and Master of the Revels. He also managed the Theatre Royal in Drury Lane.

Both brothers and their sister Anne, a Dresser to Queen Henrietta Maria, sat to Van Dyck in 1638. They make a debonair trio. All three have wide-set intelligent eyes, pointed noses and sensitive fingers. Noble and confident, their fine clothes enhance their bearing. Anne, who points to a rose-bush beside an urn, wears a lustrous gold satin dress with a grey scarf tied across her breast; William, the most serious of the three, is dressed in sober black, while Thomas, who fondles a huge mastiff, wears a breastplate and crimson sash to offset his long golden hair. Like so many of Van Dyck's sitters, they occupy with easy grace a glittering stage, unaware that the play is about to end.

p107*   Mary Grenville, as she was born, was the great-granddaughter of Sir Bevil Grenville of Stowe, who was killed during the Civil War. Her parents were grand but poor, so Mary was sent to Whitehall as a child to stay with her uncle George who was made Lord Lansdowne in 1711. His wife had been Maid of Honour to Queen Mary and was a friend of Queen Anne. With such connections young Mary would be seen, admired, and eventually wooed, it was hoped, by a rich suitor. The death of Queen Anne in 1714 put an end to these hopes. Lord Lansdowne was imprisoned in the Tower with Lord Oxford for expressing his Jacobite sympathies, and Mary and her parents fled to Buckland in Gloucestershire. Knowing that they would not be welcome at the new Hanoverian Court, and poorer than ever, the question of finding a husband for Mary, now fifteen, loomed large. On his release from prison two years later, her uncle George engineered her betrothal to an old political ally, Alexander Pendarves, who happened also to have quarrelled with his nephew and heir, Francis Basset of Tehidy, because he refused on his inheritance to adopt the name Pendarves. That he was sixty years old, exceedingly unkempt and afflicted with gout did not matter. Mary would be sure of a fortune after his death.

Mary took one look at his 'large unwieldy person, his crimson countenance' and formed an instant aversion to him. She was well aware, however, of her father's financial straits and of his debt to her uncle, who had paid him an allowance for years, and she accepted her fate with as much patience as she could muster. But although Alexander was kind to her she could not overcome her dislike of him. The couple made a slow progress down to Cornwall, staying with friends on the way. After a tiring, uncomfortable journey made almost unbearable by the proximity of her husband, they arrived at Roscrow. At first sight of her new home, Mary 'fell into a violent passion of crying'. It must have appeared to her as the back of beyond.

p108*   After eight years she was left a widow, and not a rich one, for Pendarves had lost part of his fortune in the South Sea Bubble catastrophe and part of it drinking and gambling. Nor had he altered his will, and his nephew Francis Basset inherited Roscrow after all.

p117*   After the Restoration, Francis's son Sidney entered the royal household as a page and quickly won a reputation for honesty and financial acumen. He became Lord High Treasurer under Queen Anne and was created 1st Earl of Godolphin. Margaret Godolphin, his wife, died tragically young, and there is a moving account by the diarist John Evelyn of her last journey to Cornwall, to be buried at the family home. After describing the number of the entourage, and the various stages of the long passage by road, he concludes, 'The funeral can not have cost much less than £1,000.' Godolphin's political career came to an end in 1710 when he was dismissed after the Queen's quarrel with his friend the Duke of Marlborough, whose military campaigns he had financed. As Godolphin power and influence declined, so did the house. Sidney's only son Francis, 2nd Earl of Godolphin, married Henrietta Churchill, the Duke of Marlborough's eldest daughter, and they lived mostly at Newmarket since he was passionately fond of racing.

The famous Godolphin Arab, shown in the painting by John Wootton which hangs in the dining-room belonged to him.

Four of their five children died without issue, leaving Mary, the youngest, as successor. In 1766 Mary married Thomas Osborne, the 4th Duke of Leeds, who changed his name to Godolphin-Osborne. Their heirs never lived in Cornwall.

p118* The occupations of Pengersick were perhaps not only defensive, to judge by the *St Anthony* affair. A ship of this name, a carrack of the King of Portugal, carrying a priceless cargo, was wrecked at Gunwalloe in 1526. The cargo vanished mysteriously as soon as the ship went aground, and became the subject of a Royal Commission. The first John Milliton's son, another John, together with William Godolphin and an unnamed neighbour, were implicated in the affair, but it seems no evidence was found to prove their involvement. John later became High Sheriff and Captain of St Michael's Mount – honourable positions for an honourable man. The *St Anthony*'s treasure was never recovered.

p122* Evidence exists of a flourishing trade between the Mount and the Continent. Diodorus, a Sicilian Greek historian writing early in the first century AD, quotes extracts from a lost account of a voyage made round Spain and up to Britain in the fourth century BC by a Greek geographer called Pytheas, who was searching for the source of amber in the Baltic. 'The inhabitants of that part of Britain which is called Belerion [i.e. Land's End],' says Diodorus,

are fond of strangers and from their intercourse with foreign merchants are civilised in their manner of life. They prepare the tin, working very carefully the earth in which it is produced. . . They beat the metal into masses and carry it off to a certain island off Britain called Ictis. During the ebb of the tide the intervening space is left dry and they carry over to the island the tin in abundance in their wagons.

St Michael's Mount was probably the ancient island of Ictis (the only other, less likely, alternative being the Isle of Wight), and it was no doubt the Veneti, a powerful seafaring tribe from Brittany, who carried the tin over to Gaul in sturdy ships of oak with high prows and leather sails. Having reached the mouth of the Garonne (present-day Bordeaux) they travelled overland on horseback to the Mediterranean ports of Narbonne and Marseilles. Julius Caesar's destruction of the Veneti in a mighty naval battle off Brittany in 56 BC put an end to Cornish trading and cultural links with the Continent. The Romans found another source of tin in Spain, and for a period of almost eight hundred years Cornwall was a remote backwater largely unaware of the benefits Roman civilisation had brought to the rest of Britain and unaffected by subsequent Saxon plunder.

p122* The monastery never became a centre of learning and culture like its French counterpart, partly because during the Hundred Years' War the Abbot and his monks, having sworn an oath of allegiance to Mont St Michel, were viewed with great suspicion and their revenues were often seized by the crown. Nor did the priory escape the ravages of the Black Death in 1349. By 1362 there were only two surviving monks and the prior in the monastery.

p123* Apart from its importance as a trading centre and place of pilgrimage, St Michael's Mount played its part in England's political history. In 1193, when Richard Coeur de Lion was imprisoned in Austria, having been captured by a fellow crusader on his way back from the third crusade, Henry de la Pomeray seized and occupied the Mount in the name of King Richard's brother John, Earl of Cornwall. Pomeray requested the unsuspecting monks to open the gates so that he could visit his sister in the monastery. Once inside, he and his men threw off their pilgrims' habits and forced the monks to give them possession of the various houses on the island. They lived there in style for some time, not thinking that King Richard would be ransomed for £100,000 and would return to London. At first Pomeray refused to surrender, but when an angry army arrived to besiege the Mount he gave himself up, dying, some say, of fright.

p123** It was crucial for the Mount to be in loyal and trusted hands. As a military outpost at the most south-westerly tip of England it played a vital role in both attack and defence, when a hostile force approached by sea. In 1587 the beacon seen blazing from the church tower was the first of a chain of fires to warn of the approach of the mighty Spanish Armada.

Towards the end of her reign, Queen Elizabeth, in desperate need of funds to pay for the costly Spanish wars, sold the Mount to the Earl of Salisbury. In 1640 it was sold again to a staunch Royalist, Francis Basset, a portly but dependable cavalier to judge from the fine portrait of him by Cornelis Janssens which hangs in the Mount Museum today. The Bassets were an old and respected Cornish family who had lived at the manor of Tehidy, near Camborne, since the year 1200. Francis Basset strengthened the fortifications at his own expense and left his wife Anne in charge of the Mount when he went away to fight in the Civil War. Royalist ships that had managed to escape the guns of the Parliamentarian naval blockade brought ammunition from France into the friendly waters of Mount's Bay, such arms being paid for by the sale of Cornish tin. In 1644 the young Prince of Wales lodged at the Mount on his way to the Scilly Isles.

For a few years the Mount was safe, but Royalist fortunes turned in 1645. The Cornish troops, war-weary and embittered by their own squabbling commanders, looked in admiration at Cromwell's disciplined Model Army and lost their will to fight. Soon afterwards Parliamentary troops landed in a gap between the cliffs now known as Cromwell's passage. On April 23rd, 1646, Sir Arthur Basset, Francis's brother, surrendered. Relieved at being spared a long siege, the Parliamentary army allowed Basset and his officers to retreat to the Scilly Isles.

Some Royalist leaders chose exile rather than submission to Parliament; those who remained risked having their estates confiscated and were forced to pay huge fines. Many families were ruined and the impoverished Bassets sold the Mount in 1659 to Colonel John St Aubyn, the Parliamentary leader who had been nominated Captain of the Mount twelve years earlier.

Alphabetical List of Places